THE POWER OF GOD'S CHARACTER

Don Clowers

All Scripture quotations from the King James Version, Amplified (Lockman & Zondervan), Living Bible

Amplified Bible, New Testament, Copyright © 1954, 1958 by the Lockman Foundation, © 1965 by Zondervan Publishing House. Used by permission.

The Living Bible, Copyright © 1971 Tyndale House Publishers, Wheaton, IL. Used by permission.

ISBN 0-914307-14-2

**Printed in the United States of America
Copyright © 1983 WORD OF FAITH PUBLISHING
PO Box 819000, Dallas, Texas 75381
All Rights Reserved**

Cover Photo by Doug Frame - WORD OF FAITH

TABLE OF CONTENTS

FORWARD
INTRODUCTION
Chapter 1	Compassion and Prayer	1
Chapter 2	The Character of God	5
Chapter 3	Joy is Love's Strength	9
Chapter 4	Peace is Love's Security	13
Chapter 5	Longsuffering is Love's Patience	21
Chapter 6	Gentleness is Love's Conduct	29
Chapter 7	Goodness is Love's Character	37
Chapter 8	Faith is Love's Confidence	43
Chapter 9	Meekness is Love's Humility	51
Chapter 10	Temperance is Love's Victory	61
Chapter 11	The Holy Spirit	69
Chapter 12	Concerning Gifts	89
Chapter 13	The Word of Wisdom	101
Chapter 14	The Word of Knowledge	109
Chapter 15	The Gift of Discerning of Spirits	117
Chapter 16	The Gift of Faith	125
Chapter 17	The Gift of Working of Miracles	137
Chapter 18	The Gifts of Healing	141
Chapter 19	The Gift of Prophecy	155
Chapter 20	Divers Kinds of Tongues and Interpretation of Tongues	163
Chapter 21	The Ministry Gifts	173
Chapter 22	The Ministry of an Apostle	185
Chapter 23	The Ministry of the Prophet	195
Chapter 24	The Ministry of the Evangelist	205
Chapter 25	The Ministry of a Pastor	211
Chapter 26	The Ministry of the Teacher	223

INTRODUCTION

My ministry began in 1958 at the age of 15, even though I had very little knowledge of God's Word. My life up to that point had been typical of those raised in a Christian home. I was born again as a child. My family had prayer together every night, and we attended the Pentecostal church regularly.

Before actually taking my first step into the ministry, I had been experiencing a strong craving on the inside of me to preach God's Word for quite some time. Even after receiving the baptism of the Holy Spirit as a teenager though, my life fluctuated from victory to total despair.

All of this began to change one night when the pastor gave an altar call at the end of his sermon. Almost before I knew it, I was at the altar repenting--just as I had done countless times before. Only this time there was a difference. As I poured out my soul before the Lord that night, I decided to see myself as a loser no more. From that point forward, I was determined to be an overcomer...a champion...a winner. My mind, heart, and soul were focused toward victory.

The Power Of God's Character

Even though I had never been taught about righteousness, according to Second Corinthians 5:21, or the revelation of no condemnation, according to Romans 8:1, I did not waver.

While I knelt at the altar that night, Nelson Patterson, the Youth Director of the church, prayed with me. Afterward, I began to share with him the frustration I had been experiencing, of going from the valley to the mountaintop and back in a seemingly endless cycle. I also told him I had determined in my heart to live a life of freedom, and that I had been called to preach the Gospel.

Upon hearing this, he immediately asked me to speak in the youth service the following Sunday night. I didn't know the first thing about preparing a sermon, so I began to pray and fast and seek direction from the Lord.

The whole situation became very frustrating as the Sunday night deadline drew closer and closer. I telephoned Nelson and told him I was stagnated in my sermon preparation; I couldn't even find a subject on which to speak. He gave me some advice, and was even kind enough to help me write a sermon outline. I put the sermon together quickly, but it seemed as if something was missing. For some reason, knowing that Nelson had given me the outline caused me to feel uncomfortable about it. So I called him again and told him that I had to write my own sermon. There was only one thing I knew anything about--being a backslider--so that was the subject I chose for my sermon.

Sunday night came only too quickly, and it was time for me to make my debut in the ministry by delivering my sermon on backsliding. There was a large audience that night. Knowing that didn't do anything to help my trembling voice or knocking knees. Somehow, by the grace of God, I managed to deliver my entire message.

Afterward, everyone came up, shook my hand, and told me what a great job I had done in the pulpit that night. I felt in my heart that it hadn't been all that great, but I had accomplished a major feat--I had made a start.

There was no stopping me then. I came from a large family of eight children, and I was very limited in what I could do financially, because of my father's moderate income. I knew there wasn't any way my parents could afford to send me to Bible school, so I decided to conduct my own Bible school. My "classes" were mostly at night—just me and the Holy Ghost—listening to great men of God on the radio, studying the scriptures into the wee hours of the morning, and reading every book pertaining to spiritual things that I could get my hands on.

The center of my attention was in learning how to bring help and healing to the hurting people in the world. I listened to anything, read anything, and did anything, if I thought it would help equip me with God's power. I had tremendous zeal, but very little knowledge of how to do the job God had called me to do. Nevertheless, my thirst was not quenched by the lack of knowledge or the mistakes I made.

I kept the faith and pressed on through every obstacle. I desired more than anything else in the world for God's power to be present in my life. I prayed for it, fasted for it, I craved it endlessly, especially when I listened to great men of God on the radio and heard of the miracles that were taking place in their crusades. I read Luke 4:18;

> *The Spirit of the Lord is upon me, because he hath anointed me to preach the gospel to the poor; he hath sent me to heal the brokenhearted, to preach deliverance to the captives, and recovering of sight to the blind, to set at liberty them that are bruised.* (Luke 4;18)

I read that over and over again. I got so excited about helping people that I would see myself reaching multitudes.

In retrospect, I can remember many disappointments and times of discouragement. I didn't always know how to deal with them properly, because I lacked any formal training concerning the ministry. But even with that, my compassion for people, coupled with my prayer life, brought revelation truth to me from God.

Since that first night behind the pulpit at the age of 15, God has supernaturally directed my steps, leading me into more than 40 foreign countries where I have preached in large crusades. In the U.S. I have ministered in large tent meetings and convention services countless times, and I am presently pastoring a vibrant and growing New Testament church.

It is my desire to share with you some of the experiences I have had, as well as the knowledge I gained from them, in the pages of this book. I do this so you may learn the ways of God and more rapidly comprehend how to be sensitive to the gifts of the Spirit. With these ends in mind, you and I can do a quick work together to see Jesus come after His church.

Chapter 1

COMPASSION AND PRAYER

A major lesson I learned as a teenager searching for the things of God was that I needed to have compassion—the God-kind of compassion which comes from His heart.

I frequently studied the miracles that Jesus performed, as recorded in the Gospels. One day the Holy Spirit drew me to one particular verse of scripture concerning the motivation behind Jesus' working of miracles.

And Jesus went forth, and saw a great multitude, and was moved with compassion toward them, and he healed their sick. (Matthew 14:14)

While I meditated on this and similar scriptures, a desire to lay hands on the lame, the blind, and those with all manner of diseases began to kindle within me. This

The Power Of God's Character

was not for the reason of being "God's man of power for the hour", but was a true desire to see men and women set free from the influence of Satan. As I thought about the many people in this world I saw suffering, the prayer of intercession would begin to well up out of my spirit. Many times I prayed for hours without ceasing, to learn where I could be an instrument of God's purpose for man.

You must earnestly desire the gifts of the Spirit to be able to help people, but you must also examine your motives for wanting God's power evident in your life, in the light of what the Word of God says. Is it based on compassion?

<u>Compassion united with prayer is the most effective force available to us Christians today</u>. Prayer is the communication system given by God for believers to receive from the source of life. A consistent prayer life establishes a relationship with Him and makes you realize that you do not live **for** God, but rather, you live **with** God. Prayer should not be viewed as an obligation, because you are a Christian, but as an opportunity and a privilege. No one can truly know God and understand His Word apart from frequent communication with Him in prayer.

David was a man after God's own heart. He was also a man of prayer. David never "put off" prayer, but rather thirsted for times of fellowship and communication with God. This is evidenced by one of the many verses in Psalms concerning his relationship with God.

As the hart panteth after the water brooks, so panteth my soul after thee, O God. (Psalm 42:1)

I rise early every morning to spend quality time in prayer. (Psalm 63:1) I have a prayer list which I go through and follow, and I pray in the Spirit according to Ephesians 6:18, *Praying always with all prayer and supplication in the Spirit, and watching thereunto with all perseverance and supplication for all saints.*

There are several things in this verse of scripture concerning prayer, but I want to emphasize only two of them. The first is "praying always." It means just that. Pray always, in every circumstance, every day.

The second is to pray "for all saints." God wants us to pray more for others in the body of Christ than for those in our own little personal world. Take time each day to show real concern for others by spending time in prayer for them. Before long, you will begin to see things happen and come together in your own life.

Why does that occur? Because you employed the spiritual law of sowing and reaping. When you pray for others, God will begin to place you and your situations on the heart of persons you may not even know, and they will begin to pray for you. This time of prayer would also include listening to Him, as He will talk to you and give you revelation knowledge. You will become more and more aware of His presence within you, and the door will begin to open for the operation of the gifts of the Spirit in your life.

Compassion and prayer are the prerequisites to being a successful Christian and minister of the gospel today, because they remove selfishness. Christians who allow themselves to be controlled by either their emotions or by selfishness will never be in a position to have the supernatural gifts of God flow through them in an effective manner.

I admonish you to spend quality time with God in prayer every day. It is good to pray in tongues on your way to work, or on your way home. But more than that is required, if you want to be successful in the ministry, or in your daily walk with God. You must be committed to separating yourself, in order to be alone with Him.

Chapter 2

THE CHARACTER OF GOD

In order to comprehend the operation of the gifts of the Spirit, you must first study and understand the fruit of the (human) spirit. The fruit of the spirit is the character of God, while the gifts of the Holy Spirit are the power of God.

Of these two, the first that must be developed and cultivated in your life is the fruit of the (human) spirit. Otherwise, you will not be able to operate scripturally and accurately in the demonstration of God's power through the gifts of the Spirit.

In this book you will learn how the fruit of the spirit, the gifts of the Spirit, and the fivefold ministry gifts work hand-in-hand to equip you and those you will feed for the work of the ministry.

You are a spirit; you have a soul; and you live in a body. (1st Thessalonians 5:23) It is the spirit of man, and the phenomenal events that occur in the spirit, that are usually emphasized when one speaks of a person being born again. When one's spirit is born again, it is recreated and endowed with the fullness of God.

These things that happen within the spirit are astonishing, but the soul of man—also a part of every believer—is oftentimes overlooked. The realm of the soul includes the mind (intellect), will, and emotions. Your soul is responsible for making the decisions to walk in the ways of God, and for expressing God to the world around you. However, it does not receive an instantaneous change like that of the spirit at the new birth. Every believer must develop their own emotions, mind, and will to conform with their newly-recreated spirit. This process is a perpetual one, as the soul must be continually renewed by the Word of God. This continual renewing by the Word will bring about the transformation spoken of in Romans twelve.

> *1. I beseech you therefore, brethren, by the mercies of God, that ye present your bodies a living sacrifice, holy, acceptable unto God, which is your reasonable service.*
>
> *2. And be not conformed to this world: but be ye transformed by the renewing of your mind, that ye my prove what is that good, and acceptable, and perfect will of God.* (Romans 12:1-2)

Second Corinthians 5:15 says, "All those who live might live no longer to and for themselves, but to and with Him Who died and Who was raised again." **(paraphrased)**

What does this mean? It means, once you are recreated in your spirit by the new birth, you no longer live for yourself. Your will must conform to God's will. Your mind should choose compassion over selfishness; meekness over pride. You must allow the love that God has emplanted into your spirit to begin to be demonstrated in your thoughts, and ultimately, in your actions. You must let the love which is in your spirit flow into your soul, where it can touch the lives of those around you.

22. But the fruit of the spirit is love, joy, peace, longsuffering, gentleness, goodness, faith,

23. Meekness, temperance: against such there is no law. (Galatians 5:22-23)

Notice in particular that verse 22 speaks of the fruit of the spirit, not the fruits—it is singular. Love is the fruit. Joy, peace, longsuffering, gentleness, goodness, faith, meekness and temperance are by-products of that love. Every believer should endeavor to become love-inspired, love-motivated and love-driven. Without the fruit of the spirit being developed in their emotions, they are just a religious noise. The fruit of the spirit is love, and it is expressed through the emotions in love. A spirit-controlled person—who is actually a love-controlled person—needs no law to cause him to live a righteous life.

As has been mentioned before in Romans 12, you must present yourself unto God continually, so that His love may continue to flow through you. Only as you live a life that is love-centered can you fulfill the will of God in your life.

Chapter 3

JOY IS LOVE'S STRENGTH

You cannot have joy unless you first have love on the inside of you—in your spirit. Joy is an expression of God's love through your emotions. Nehemiah 8:10 says, *"The joy of the Lord is my strength."* Joy is love's strength.

You can be a joyful Christian if you learn how to draw from the love of God that's in your spirit. Christians who have no joy have never learned to live in the Spirit. Remember, your soulish realm must be in tune with the spirit-man that's within you.

Joy is defined as... " a very glad feeling."

In recent years, those of us who have been in the faith message have been taught that we are not supposed to be moved by what we see or feel. Therefore, many of us have come to the conclusion that there is no place for feelings or emotions in the Christian life.

This is not true. We have feelings because we have emotions. How does joy, or a glad feeling, come? It comes by applying the scriptures to our lives, instead of talking about how bad everything is. Philippians 4:4 says, *Rejoice in the Lord alway: and again I say, Rejoice.* In other words, don't allow your emotions to control you. Instead, you control them.

A knowledge of the scripture is important in maintaining joy in one's life. However, that's not enough. The Bible says, *"the letter (of the Law) killeth, but the spirit giveth life."* (2nd Corinthians 3:6)

Spiritual things should not be judged according to the amount of emotion that was either displayed or restrained. People get in Full Gospel circles and have the impression that unless they have strong emotion, nothing much is going to happen.

This is a deception. Emotions are important, but not primary. Man is an emotional being, and if the emotions are stifled or bottled up and no expression is given to them, that person is living a stunted life. It's unnatural, and the result will be some kind of inward wound, sooner or later.

Why?

Because what you stifle continues to work inside of you, but only in a negative way. Your emotions can control you and cause you to miss God, or you can control your emotions and follow God. Joy is from God, but there are times when you must do all you know to do in order to experience that joy.

A particular instance of a time such as this stands out in my memory. It was June first, 1982. My fifteen-year-old son, Jeff, had been helping me do some work around the church that day. During the course of the day, we found him lying on the floor, dead . . . electrocuted. He had been with Jesus for several hours before we discovered him. My wife and I loved Jeff very much and were looking forward to sharing everything we knew about the ministry with him. I had often looked forward to helping bring into reality the calling God had on his life.

All at once, however, the dreams I had dreamed were gone forever. Never again could my wife or I ever touch or see our son Jeff in this life.

Can you imagine the pain and sorrow that we felt? It was almost unbearable. Praise God, He has a reciprocal for pain and sorrow—and that reciprocal is **JOY!** Every day we relied on God by meditating, thinking and talking about the things that made us joyful.

Although we felt bitterness, along with many other emotions, we knew we had to control our emotions, rather than allowing our emotions to control us. We not only cried, but we also rejoiced that Jeff was in the presence of God, and no longer had to fight the fight of faith. There were times when both my wife Sharon and I wanted to die, even though we had each other and three other wonderful children. But we dealt with that emotion and brought a good and glad feeling into our souls, rather than giving in to what we felt.

When a man is gloomy, everything seems to go wrong; when he is cheerful, everything seems to go right. (Proverbs 15:15 Living)

We could have given in to the gloomy feelings we felt, but we made the decision to be cheerful so that the rest of our lives would go right, and so we could minister more effectively to hurting people.

Remember, you must choose to let joy come forth, regardless of the circumstance. Joy is rejoicing continually in the Lord in the midst of one's problems. You must learn to rule your attitudes and not let them rule you.... *Weeping may endure for a night, but joy cometh in the morning* (Psalm 30:5).

How?

By speaking the Words of God and drawing from that divine love that is on the inside of you. You can't have real joy until you have the real love of God being released in your emotions.

Begin training your emotions to rejoice. Even in the hours of the hardest times, you can have joy. You **can** have strength! You might cry through tragedy and pain, but at the same time you can have true joy. I know this is true, because I've experienced it. Pray in tongues; sing songs of praise; utter positive words. If you feel as if you can't utter positive words, then pray in tongues and build yourself up until you can. The love of God in your spirit can flow into your emotions and cause you to become strong. It caused Paul to say, *I can do all things through Christ who strengthens me* (Philippians 4:13).

You cannot be effective in the gifts of the Spirit unless you are joyful and excited. You can't fake joy, or put it on—it has to be **real.** Can you imagine going to the altar for prayer, needing ministry, desperately needing a word of wisdom, or a miracle, or healing for your body, and the minister who meets you there is sad and depressed?

No. The gifts of the Spirit won't operate under such circumstances. The gifts of the Spirit are for edification and comfort. Therefore, it is important for you to express joy at all times.

Chapter 4

PEACE IS LOVE'S SECURITY

Peace is a by-product of love. If you have God's peace permeating your emotions, it is originating out of His divine love that was imparted to your spirit at the new birth. The dictionary definition of peace is "an undisturbed state of mind; the absence of mental conflict; serenity; calmness; quietness; tranquility." When attacks of Satan come, as a believer, you must decide for yourself whether you are going to have turmoil or tranquility.

Being born-again does not cause your mind to be problem-free. You will definitely have problems as long as you live in this life. But it does not mean that you are saved to tribulate. When problems do arise, you can experience calmness and quietness of mind by calling upon the love of God that's inside of you. If you are fighting the good fight of faith concerning your finances, yet your thoughts are telling you there is no way that you are going to make it--you need peace and tranquillity of mind. If you didn't have obstacles to overcome, then you wouldn't need peace in your mind. When everything in your life is going well, things are calm. But when trouble starts, you need to keep an undisturbed state of mind, rather than permitting Satan to move you. Having a tranquil mind allows you to see your situation the same way God sees it--as a winner and conqueror over the circumstances, because Satan is a defeated foe.

Jesus said,

These things I have spoken unto you, that in me ye might have peace. In the world ye shall have tribulation: but be of good cheer; I have overcome the world. (John 16:33)

The word "peace" in this verse is the Greek word "serene", meaning "rest; quietness." God wants you to rest, or to be calm in Him--to trust Him.

When I lie down on my bed at night, I never check to see if it's capable of supporting my weight.

Why? Because I trust it.

That's why you need to develop peace in your daily life--so that whether good things or bad things occur, you automatically and spontaneously rest in God's Word.

Jesus said,

Come unto me, all ye that labour and are heavy laden, and I will give you rest. (Matthew 1:28)

The word "rest" in this verse could have easily been translated "peace," as they are synonymous in the origi-

Peace is Love's Security

nal Greek text.

You **can** have peace. If you meditate on doubt and dwell on unbelief, you are doing so to your detriment.

Colossians 3:15 says, *"let the peace of God rule in your hearts."* The term "hearts" in this verse means your thoughts, or your mind. You must choose to have God's peace in your mind, rather than turmoil; and then develop that peace.

One night as Sharon and I were driving home from a meeting, my mind became troubled by some circumstances which we were facing. The night before, I had allowed Satan to steal my peace, causing me not to sleep the entire night. I shared with Sharon how I felt, and what was going on inside of me.

She said, "Don, you are worrying. There is no peace in worry. Worry is fear of bad things, or meditating on things that you don't want to happen. You don't have to walk in fear. Fear is in your emotions--it's the opposite of faith. It doesn't matter what is happening around us, you can have peace, in Jesus' Name."

Then she laid her hands on me and said, "I rebuke the spirit of fear; and I command you, Don, to have peace."

Almost immediately I began to laugh. I experienced peace of mind. The pressure was gone. I had won the victory over fear, just as God said I could.

I learned a lesson that day that I have never forgotten--I don't have to live under pressure. I can live in peace, because I am God's child. I can experience the God-kind of life that is filled with peace.

> *And the peace of God, which passeth all understanding, shall keep your hearts and minds through Christ Jesus.* (Philippians 4:7)

What shall keep your mind? Love, demonstrated through peace. Sometimes you are kept by the peace of God, and it's above your understanding. But nevertheless, you just rest in that peace. The very next verse of scripture contains another golden nugget concerning peace:

> *Finally, brethren, whatsoever things are true, ...honest, ...just, ...pure, ...lovely, ...of good report; if there be any virtue, and if there be any praise, think on these things.* (Philippians 4:8)

If you want to have peace, you have to think on good things. You have to think on things that have life and virtue. In order to maintain peace, you must think on the things that produce life. Thinking of the worst thing that could happen in any situation, and preparing yourself for it ahead of time does not cause peace to be present in your heart and mind. I have heard people say, "I always prepare for the worst. Then, if something good happens, I'm not disappointed."

This is the world's way, because they have no hope. And because they have no hope, they have no peace.

God's Word tells you to do just the opposite--to be prepared for the best. Then if disappointment does occur, you are not to be disturbed by it. You must stay calm until you see the end result that God has promised.

Several years ago, my ministry gift was that of an evangelist. I traveled across the United States conducting revivals and crusades using a tent. At one particular point during this time, the tent I was using had grown too small for the size of audience I was drawing on a regular basis. I learned of a much larger tent that was for sale by another evangelist, and I decided to buy it. The selling price was $10,000, with $1,000 deposit, and 10 days to clear the balance.

At that time in my ministry, that was an extremely large sum for me to acquire in such a short period of time. I took the step though, believing God to meet the need.

By the ninth day, only $2,500 had been received in the offerings. I needed $6,500 more, but I did not become disturbed. God's Word was the foundation I stood upon, and I had cast the care of the situation on Him, according to First Peter 5:7.

That night I was called to minister at a small church nearby. God moved mightily, yet the offering was minimal. I continued not being moved by that seemed to be an impossible situation.

A couple who knew me and followed me to some of my meetings came up after the service and asked me to go out with them. I did, and during the course of conversation, they related to me that God had been speaking to them about helping my ministry financially.

They told me that they didn't have much; **only $6,500** to sow into the ministry.

My reaction must have shocked them. The joy that I felt at God meeting the need to the exact dollar was almost uncontainable. There was no way they could have known the amount desired, as I had not shared it with anyone but my family and staff.

During the entire time, I had peace. The reason was that I did not meditate on what I would do if the deposit money was lost, but rather, I meditated on receiving the money to obtain a needed ministry tool.

A similar event occurred after I began pastoring. In keeping with the fulfillment of the vision God gave to me for the city of Chattanooga, I had been searching for land which would be used for the World Outreach Center. I had traveled all over the city. Many empty church buildings and small parcels of land were considered; some with the idea of "This must be the one, Lord!" But none bore witness inside of me.

Then through a friend I learned of a 25 acre tract of land in the area I had desired. After riding over the acreage in its entirety and claiming it for the Lord, He spoke to me that this was it.

A contract was signed, a $10,000 deposit was placed, and closing was scheduled 90 days from then. I did not anticipate any problems in obtaining the balance of $240,000 from the bank which I had dealt with for the past twenty years, as the land had appraised for much more than the selling price.

But to my surprise, they turned me down flat with very little explanation. I contacted every other lending institution I knew of, with the same result. The devil was really fighting this step of faith.

As the day to close loomed closer and closer, nothing had changed. I called a meeting of the men of the church, and some men who were not members, but were interested in our ministry. I explained things, and told them the situation had been carried as far as I could take it, and the result was up to God.

I had total peace about it. After the meeting was over, a man came up to me and told me, "You don't know it,

Peace is Love's Security

but I hold one of the mortgages on that property, and the Lord has spoken to me to release that to the church."

After rejoicing heartily in the Lord, we looked at the amount; it was more than $32,000. The man not only did that, but he also introduced me to the lending institution that would give us the remaining financing. The Lord worked for me, because His Word promised that He would. And the supernatural peace He gave to me during a time of what could have been extreme stress was a testimony to all concerned.

If you really believe God's Word, peace becomes your security whenever troubles or attacks of Satan come. You can stand secure in God's Word and not be disturbed by the bad things that happen around you.

For to be carnally minded is death; but to be spiritually minded is life and peace. (Romans 8:6)

The word "life" in this scripture means the God-kind of peace-filled life that you receive when you think on the things of God. The more you discipline yourself to pray and meditate on His Word, the more His life will flow through you--producing peace.

I call heaven and earth to record this day against you, that I have set before you life and death, blessing and cursing: therefore choose life, that both thou and thy seed may live. (Deuteronomy 30:19)

My wife and I have had a lot of tragedy occur around us since we were married, but we live tranquil lives. We are not paranoid every time the phone rings. We could live in fear, but we choose to let peace be at work in us.

20

Chapter 5

LONGSUFFERING IS LOVE'S PATIENCE

Longsuffering in the Greek means "forbearance, fortitude or patience." Many times, as you go through situations, you find yourself having patience and strength that you never knew you had.

And not only so, but we glory in tribulations also: knowing that tribulation worketh patience. (Romans 5:3)

It doesn't say that tribulations give you patience. Patience is derived from the fruit of the spirit, which is love. You have within you the ability to be patient during tribulations, trials, and tests. When your patience begins to be applied, then you obtain experience. You learn to tackle Satan head-on, because you have had experience with him before. You know you are able to use the Word of

The Power Of God's Character

God against him again and again. Patience is the quality that does not surrender to circumstances nor succumb under trial. Patience is the opposite of despondancy, and is associated with hope. If you lose your hope or your vision, there is nothing for your faith to work toward.

I have developed a great amount of patience over the years. I'm a winner. I'm a fighter. I see only the end result. The worse a situation looks, the stronger I become, because I keep my eye on the vision.

Once a man came up to me and gave me the keys to a truck. He told me that along with the truck came a beautiful stallion and a trailer. He declined to tell me though, that the horse was not saddle-broken. So I placed a saddle on the horse, and he appeared to tolerate it quite well. Not having ridden a great deal, I gingerly placed my foot in the left stirrup. That horse didn't move. As I began to place my weight on my left foot and swing my right one over, it seemed as if I had stepped into the middle of a heavyweight boxing match. Before I knew it, I was flat on my back on the ground, looking up at that horse. I got up, brushed myself off, and spoke to that horse: "Tex, you're not getting away with that!"

Again I placed my left foot into the stirrup; but this time I mounted him so quickly he didn't have time to throw me off. Immediately my thoughts began to tell me that I had made the wrong decision, as I looked and felt like a rag doll in a dryer. That horse bucked up, down, frontward, backward, and side-to-side, but I held on. Just before I thought I couldn't hold on any longer, He began to settle down.

Tex wasn't completely broken then. It took more rides similar to that one; yet each one was less intense.

This occurred because I was determined to be patient with him.

You don't pray for patience. If I had just prayed for patience in that instance and the succeeding ones, I would have been doing so flat on my back. No, I developed more patience by exercising it, the same way a bodybuilder develops his muscles.

Patience is the difference between trying and doing. Some people say, "I'll try it for a while."

That is not enough. Don't be a tryer of the Word; be a doer. Lack of patience is one of the major causes of failure. Satan would love to have you concede to his bluff and give up. There is something worse than losing or falling, and that is never making an effort at all. Proverbs 24:16 says that a righteous man may fall seven times, but he gets up again.

The preparation for continuing to use and build your patience is found in Second Timothy four.

Preach the word; be instant in season, out of season; reprove, rebuke, exhort with all longsuffering and doctrine. (2nd Timothy 4:2)

Be ready at all times to use the Word of God to move circumstances, instead of allowing them to move you.

...that whosoever shall say unto this mountain, be thou removed, and be thou cast into the sea; and shall not doubt in his heart, but shall believe that those things which he saith shall come to pass; he shall have whatsoever he saith. (Mark 11:23)

Some say, "That's easy for you to say, but not so easy to do."

This is true, but have you ever thought about the fact that there are different-sized mountains? The smaller ones move fairly easily and quickly. The larger ones take longer. The position of any mountain has never been changed, though, until that mountain is removed. Patience is the force that keeps the shovel moving.

The "all" in being ready at all times to speak and do God's Word does not mean "just when it is convenient." There are times when you feel strong emotionally, and times when you do not. As David encouraged himself in the Lord during a time when even his most loyal followers wanted to stone him (1st Samuel 30:6), you are to do accordingly. If you have a vision, and put your faith out for a particular area of achievement concerning that vision, but fail to accomplish it, **don't give up!** Instead, remain patient and stand for something better.

Remember, Satan comes to kill, to steal, and to destroy. (John 10:10) He wants to steal the seed of the Word out of your heart through affliction, persecution, the cares of this world, the deceitfulness of riches, and the lusts of the flesh. Joshua was patient. He walked around the walls of Jericho once a day for six days, but on the seventh day he marched around the wall seven times, and then began to shout. Do you remember what happened? God gave them the city.

Don't let yourself deviate away from what God has said. Let patience have its perfect work.

Hebrews 6:12 says, *"That ye be not slothful, but followers of them who through faith and patience inherit the promises."* Some want faith overnight, but it takes patience to inherit the promises of God. Sometimes, Satan will repeatedly tell you that you will not get an answer to your prayers. In the event this occurs, find someone who has had success in the area of your prayers, and begin thanking God for their victory. Then tell Satan that God is not a respecter of persons; what He has done for this other person, He will do for you.

God does answer instantly, but the majority of the time, you receive your answers according to your level of faith in the Word of God. You must allow time for your seeds to come up properly, in God's timing. Some think God gives out blessings in the way that a fast food chain operates; drive up to a remote speaker, recite your order, pay your money, and pick up what was ordered almost immediately.

This is a deception. First of all, God tells you to make your requests known **to Him**, not to a third party. Next, you are absolutely unable to purchase any blessing from God. You sow in faith and receive by grace. Last, there is a certain minimum time period between the time you sow and the time the planted seed comes up to be reaped. The length of that minimum is relative to your level of faith. Patience keeps faith applied while the Word is bringing about the manifestation of your request.

For ye have need of patience, that, after ye have done the will of God, ye might receive the promise. (Hebrews 10:36)

When do you receive the promise?

After you have done the will of God! Are you saying, "But I've done everything I know to do, and it's not working"? Then hold on and give it time. If you have trouble in the area of patience, meditate on how corn grows. First

The Power Of God's Character

the blade, then the ear, and after that the full corn in the ear. There is a time to plant seed, and there is the growing time. You have to learn to be patient during growing time.

A classic example of the result of patience is found in the Chinese bamboo tree. It is one of two thousand different types of bamboo trees, but it has a unique feature. When the seed is first planted, it is watered and fertilized. Then it is left alone to begin to mature. After the first year, nothing seems to have happened, but the farmer waters and fertilizes it again. The same thing is done in the second, third, and fourth years. To look at the situation at face value, the seed is dead and will never grow. Yet in the fifth year, it is watered and fertilized once more. Toward the latter part of the year, something wonderful happens. Within a six-week period, the seed bursts forth from the ground and grows to a height of 60 feet or more.

Watering and fertilizing are the acts of patience needed to keep the seed alive during the period of maturation.

Many times I have been tempted to blow everything, including the harvest. But I know God's Word is true, and I know He is my Father. He has everything I need. He wants me to have all my needs met. I do my part by standing still and keeping patience working.

How?

By developing it out of love.

Hebrews 12:1 says, *"let us run with patience the race that is set before us."* If you continue walking the walk of faith, what do you have to lose? If you give up, nothing has changed anyway. By walking in faith, you keep your emotions under control--even to the point of not ever feeling sorry for yourself--which is what Satan wants you to do. Nothing can be accomplished in the kingdom of God by sitting around and having pity parties. Pity parties only make things worse; and certainly, patience can't develop in that kind of atmosphere.

Someone once told me, "You don't know what I've gone through."

My answer was, "Maybe not, but Jesus went through it all."

So stand up, exercise your patience, and become strong in every area of your life.

3 Knowing this, that the trying of your faith worketh patience.

4 But let patience have her perfect work, that ye may be perfect and entire, wanting nothing. (James 1:3-4)

James is saying, if you develop your patience, you will be mature and wanting nothing, because you know that God is your source, and you are not moved by the things around you. As you develop this by-product of love in your life, you will see God at work more and more within you.

7 ...Behold, the husbandman waiteth for the precious fruit of the earth, and hath long patience for it, until he receive the early and latter rain.

8 Be ye also patient; stablish your hearts: for the coming of the Lord draweth nigh. (James

5:7-8)

What a beautiful reward for the Christian. When we are established in patience and walk the walk of faith, our needs are met according to His riches in glory (Philippians 4:19). It gives God pleasure for us to be patient and produce fruit in the earth. On the final day, He will say, *"Well done, thou good and faithful servant."*

I am looking forward to that time, but I will be patient until I get to the finish line.

Chapter 6

GENTLENESS IS LOVE'S CONDUCT

During the course of life, everyone has been programmed with strife, envy, jealousy and many other negative things. Therefore, it is impossible for the love of God to come through until the quality decision is made to be gentle--having the conduct of God, rather than what has been taught in the former environment.

Just as plants have to be cared for, watered, receive good light, so does the soul of man. The spirit is illuminated with God, but the soul has to have constant care, like a plant. Your spirit is always flowing with love, but that love will be cut off by the soul, if it is not receiving proper care.

How do you properly care for our soul?

By regularly ingesting the Word.

The Power Of God's Character

The word "gentleness" comes from the Greek word "chrestotes," and means "good, kindness, or excellence; not violent, not harsh or rough; a gentle rebuke."

You will respond in all situations with the conduct of Jesus as you train your mind, will and emotions to respond to your spirit rather than to the resent circumstance.

When you have an opportunity to overcome strife, it is not your spirit that has the problem, it is your emotions. If you are born again, your spirit has the life of God--and God does not produce strife. Your spirit cannot produce life and death at the same time. According to Proverbs 18:21, your tongue produces death or life in your soul.

Life is in your spirit, but your emotions and your will pattern after that of your master. You can only serve one master. You can either follow after God and serve Him, or follow after Satan and serve him. If you choose to serve Satan, your emotions will begin to pattern themselves after him (lying, hatred, strife, envy, etc.). However, if you choose to serve God, your emotions will begin to pattern themselves after Him (love, joy, peace, longsuffering, gentleness, goodness, faith, meekness, and temperance).

Romans 5:5 says, *the love of God is shed abroad in our hearts.* God has put His love in your spirit, but it's your responsibility to produce it in your soul.

The conduct of Christ is not a griping, hateful attitude; nor is it being tempermental or moody. There are times when many may justify acting unlike Christ, because they slipped or missed the mark.

When you do, don't blame someone else or make excuses. Repent to God and ask forgiveness of the person

Gentleness is Love's Conduct

you got into strife with right then--don't justify it. This is one sure way of keeping out of the same old rut.

My wife told me that some women think they have a right to be touchy, resentful, and just plain hard to get along with, because they are going through their monthly cycle. Women need to take God's Word and overcome these emotions during this time, even though they may not feel like being gentle and kind. The conduct of Christ is to be gentle in all things. The Word does not make exceptions.

Everything discussed up to this point has great importance concerning the operation of the gifts of the Spirit.

Why?

If you cannot handle your emotions by producing God's character, you cannot have God's power working effectively in you.

6 Similarly, encourage the young men to be self-controlled.

7 In everything set them an example by doing what is good. In your teaching show integrity, seriousness

8 and soundness of speech that cannot be condemned, so that those who oppose you may be ashamed because they have nothing bad to say about us.

9 Teach slaves to be subject to their masters in everything, to try to please them, not to talk back to them. (Titus 2:6-9 NIV)

This scripture tells us to encourage our youth to have self-control. If the parents in America would wake up and recognize the wisdom in this passage of scripture, many problems could be solved. Proverbs 22:6 says, *Train up a child in the way he should go...,* not in the things he should not do.

The church I grew up in always stressed the things I shouldn't do, rather than the things I should do. It caused me much pain, because I couldn't stand running to God when I made mistakes. Instead, I ran ran from God when I slipped and missed the mark. Often, I thought I might as well give up because I made a mistake; thus the need to always run to the altar, as I mentioned in the introduction.

As believers, you are to be examples of the conduct of Christ in everything that you do. Children should be taught about authority, and they should be disciplined.

Parents must learn to discipline their children with the right attitude, though. If the attitude is wrong, proper teaching cannot be accomplished. If parents fail to teach their children to respect authority, they will be unable to hold a job or work in a controlled environment as they grow older.

God's conduct is living like Jesus.

Have you ever known people who are on a job eight hours a day, and get paid for eight hours, but only work four hours? Get ready for this...they are stealing four hours of pay. When they tithe on that money, there is no return, because it was money that was actually stolen.

If you are on salary and you come in late or leave early, your employer may not know it, but God does. We should be like Christ, whether or not anyone is watching.

Gentleness is Love's Conduct

As a joint heir with Christ, you are to set an example by doing what is good. If you desire to be used of God in any of the gifts of the Spirit, you are to pay your bills. I can't receive from someone when I know they are ignoring their material, physical or financial responsibilities. If you agreed to a contract, you should live up to it....Jesus would.

This is a very important concept concerning how the power of God operates in our lives. If you cannot walk with Him in His character and nature, you will never demonstrate His power effectively.

It is important that husbands and wives work at being gentle with each other. Just because rough or harsh things have happened to you, that does not give you a right to be rough or harsh in return.

I want to share with you a humorous example of how we let silly disagreements which end up being strife, control our emotions. When Sharon and I married, she was 17 and I was 19. Three months after our marriage, we experienced our first disagreement. It was during the time we were holding a tent meeting in West Virginia. I don't even remember the reason for the argument, but after the evening service was over, we went home and got in bed, not saying one word to each other. I had to hold on to my side of the bed to keep from turning over and touching Sharon, and she did the same regarding me. After a night's rest, we woke up to a new day; and forgetting that we were mad at each other, we loved on each other.

Upon remembering that we had been angry, we quickly turned over, again grasping our own side of the bed. We had very quiet meals. Sharon fixed and served my meals, but not one word was spoken....nice, but quiet meals.

I was really "some kind" of an evangelist, and that was some kind" of meetings. Can you imagine it? On the way to meetings, a deafening quietness. Sharon sat as close as possible to her side of the car, and I did the same on my side. Reaching our destination, we got out of the car and went into the meeting....smiling all the way! But during the meeting, as I was preaching, I wouldn't look in the section Sharon was sitting in for anything! I was really ngry!

Then after the meetings, we quietly drove home again. Neither of us knew how long this non-sense would last. It was like we were having a contest to see which one could hold out the longest.

Sharon was so quiet, she probably would have won. But after three long, quiet days, I couldn't take it any longer. I went to Sharon and apologized, and she accepted my apology. We both promised, right there where we were, that we would never again do this to each other. We have now been married over 21 years, and it has never happened again.

Sometimes there is a true need for a rebuke within a marriage. If there needs to be a rebuke, though, it can be done at the proper time and place. One definition of gentleness is "a gentle rebuke." If you do it with the right attitude, it will work. First Peter 3:7 tells us to treat each other properly *that our prayers be not hindered*.

As long as you smart-mouth your husband or wife or child or parents, you will never be successful. Love is gentle, even when you don't feel like it. The character of

God is demonstrated through your emotions. You are the only one who decides whether you will be gentle or rash.

You can be firm and strong without getting into strife. It is really dangerous to get into strife. James 3:16 says, *For where envying and strife is, there is confusion and every evil work.*

With strife and unforgiveness, a person is open to confusion, and is not a candidate for operating in any of the gifts of the Spirit. Don't give place to the devil. Express God's conduct, and be gentle in all things.

Chapter 7

GOODNESS IS LOVE'S CHARACTER

My desire is that by the time you finish this book, your eyes will be enlightened, and you will have a greater understanding of the fact that the gifts of the Spirit are for those who set their sights on God's best, not those satisfied with being average. I want to point out to you that being Christ-like is your first responsibility. Expressing Christ in your conduct will certainly open the door for those around you to see Christ and give you an opportunity to witness to them, or even pray for them.

The Greek word translated "goodness" is defined as virtue or pure, benevolent, generous, willing to share, to give unselfishly, and compassion. It also means God-like in conduct. One of the first things you need to know in this area is how to treat other people. To have any of the gifts of the Spirit flowing through you, you must be a giv-

37

The Power Of God's Character

ing person; giving to people, not only with money, but also knowing how to serve others with joy. God loved us so much that He gave His Son; Jesus loved us so much that He gave His life. If you don't give willingly, you cannot expect the supernatural gifts of God, or any of the five ministry gifts to operate in your life.

In my teenage ministry, one of the things I enjoyed most was the opportunity to serve men of God. They were little things, but I did them as unto the Lord, and I was very pleased when I got opportunity to serve. Now that I have a successful ministry, things have not changed. I still enjoy serving, and do it at every opportunity.

Greater love hath no man than this, that a man lay down his life for his friends. (John 15:13)

This verse of scripture does not mean for you to die for someone. Jesus has already done that. The implications are this: take time out of what you are doing and help your friends; don't be selfish and only do your own thing. Gladly take time out of your schedule and help others. Rejoice at every opportunity you have to serve another child of God. Remember the law of sowing and reaping.

Luke 6:38 says, *Give and it shall be given.* It must be a gift with no strings attached. You expect nothing in return from the person you give to. God is your source, and He will supply your need through someone, but not necessarily a person you serve. If you do it expecting something in return from them, you are not giving; you are putting them in debt to you.

Owe no man anything, but to love one another: for he that loveth another hath fulfilled the law. (Romans 13:8)

Love them with deeds and action, not just words. Everywhere Jesus went, He did good. Don't serve a person or do good things for them and put them in debt to you, or go tell someone all you have done for them. If you want recognition for what you have done, you are not doing it out of love or goodness. That is not the heart of a servant. Remember, goodness is pure, virtuous and kind.

Sharon and I are givers. We made a covenant with each other from the beginning of our marriage that we would be tithers. We never took God's part and used it on ourselves or our ministry. We always gave willingly and cheerfully to others. God has always sustained us, and we have always been successful.

Early in our marriage, many of the churches in which I preached gave us very little money. This meant that we had to stay in someone's home most of the time. However, we never complained and were thankful for the provision we had. The first thing we did with our income was to take out God's part and give it to Him. We had a 1957 Chevrolet that I was making payments on. Sometimes we would travel more than a thousand miles to the next place. Most of the time we drove straight through because we didn't have the money for a motel room. We rejoiced for every open door to minister, though. We remained faithful to God with our gifts, and God gave the increase.

Develop your business first before building your house. (Proverbs 24:27 Living)

That's what we did. We gave, then God moved for us financially. Soon our income had increased to the level that we could provide for our own lodging and have our privacy. Then came a new car, a house, and much more.

Don't expect a flow of spiritual gifts, if you can't trust God and love God enough to support the Body. I'm not attempting to put you under the law with this statement; but I have had people on my staff as ministers, and they would not tithe or give of their income. Yet they wanted to be in the ministry and take from the ministry.

That is not the way it works. A person on the staff of any ministry should be a cheerful giver of their income. If they aren't, they are stopping the flow of life.

If you want to receive, you must sow; and if you don't sow goods, how can you expect anything different than what you have sown?

The conduct of Christ is kind. Don't ever look at a person in the ministry and see some bad habits they have, such as being rude or sharp with people, and justify your actions by what you have seen them do. Remember, Christ is your example. The Word is what we have to go by. Paul said in First Corinthians 11:1, *Be ye followers of me, even as I also am of Christ.* Be followers of good. The preaching and teaching of the Word is to lift you up and encourage you, not to condemn you. It will instruct you through the ways of righteousness in the way you should walk. The Word will inspire you to do good at all times, even when you are being falsely accused.

When the goodness is being applied in your life, you will be enforcing Romans 12:21, *Be not overcome with evil, but overcome evil with good.* I will agree with you that there are times when you don't feel like being good, but do it anyway. Jesus would, so let love be demonstrated into and through your emotions by showing goodness.

I was in Guatemala after an earthquake. It was one of the worst experiences I have ever had in my entire life.

Families were torn apart by disaster. Disaster camps were put together, and 5,000 people or more would be put in these places. It was terrible. We would try to witness to these people, but many of them would not listen.

Why?

Because they had been told that God did that to them. John 10:10 says Jesus came to give life, not to destroy. The thief is the killer. So what kind of an image did these people have of God? No wonder they didn't want to hear about God.

When you do good, you will produce Jesus to the world. The world cannot see our spirit, but we can see how the emotional man responds to his environment. When our emotions are being controlled, they will be an effective witness for God.

In a Full Gospel meeting that I attended, a minister called for a prayer line, and a lady with cancer responded by coming forward. The minister quoted some scripture to her and showed her that it was God's will to heal her. All at once, there was a commotion in the back of the church. A young man was crying and repenting. When he was calmed and asked what caused him to make the decision to accept Christ, he said, "Where my mother has been going to church, the minister told my mother that God had given her cancer in order to make me serve Him. Well, that only made me bitter toward God, and I would not accept Him. It drove me away from Him. When I heard the good news that God did not put this disease on her, and that it was His will to heal her, I saw God in a different light, and I wanted to serve Him."

The Power Of God's Character

I believe the areas of goodness are the areas where we must do all we know to do to express the goodness of God through our conduct.

Chapter 8

FAITH IS LOVE'S CONFIDENCE

Faith is defined as assurance, truth in itself, belief, and fidelity. I want to amplify this word **FAITH** here so you will be better able to apply it to your life. In this context, faith means faithful. God desires faithfulness in His children, but if you fall short or miss the mark, He will forgive you.

If we confess our sins, he is faithful and just to forgive us our sins, and to cleanse us from all unrighteousness. (1st John 1:9)

God will forgive you of your sins.

Why?

Because He is the faithful God. Who is He faithful to? He is faithful to Jesus. In other words, by what Jesus did at the cross, when you make a mistake and go to God asking forgiveness, you obtain it. You don't deserve it of yourself--but through Jesus you do. It's not God's best when you fall short; but if you do, you must repent--this is one of your covenant conditions.

When you are tried by the enemy, you must remain faithful to God. Don't change your mind and start in another direction because circumstances arise. Don't be distracted from your goal or your purpose. Be faithful to God.

If you want God to trust you with His power, you must trust Him. A relationship with God is two-fold. It's like a strong marriage; built on two people, not one. You see, both are trusting and loyal to each other. You must be loyal to God, even though there is opportunity to change.

Anyone who lets himself be distracted from the work I plan for him is not fit for the kingdom of God. (Luke 9:62 Living)

Here is proof that you can choose not to be distracted, but loyal and faithful to God, constant in your profession of faith. Don't let yourself be distracted from the plan and purpose God has in your life. Remain faithful (loyal) at all times.

There is one area in which I have seen many people of the Charismatic era fall down: lack of commitment to a local church and Pastor. There is no scripture to support the actions of those who will not settle down and find a church and work in it. Being loyal to that church and Pastor is very important, because if you can't work there and be faithful to the Pastor, how can God exalt you? You may have your own ministry, but you need a local Pastor to feed you and minister to you. If your ministry has reached the level where you are frequently out of town, you must, when you return, be fed by a local Pastor that you can trust.

There are many who desire to be in the full-time ministry. If God has called you to one, be faithful where you are. In other words, if you are now a Children's Ministry Pastor and you believe God has called you to pastor a church, then be faithful to that and do it with joy. Don't abuse that position. Those children have needs, and it is very important that you minister to them effectually. One of them could grow up to have a ministry like Oral Roberts.

If you are not diligent and faithful there, you are only using that position to get another one; your motives would be wrong.

I believe, though, that God calls people just to work with children, and that it is not an insignificant ministry. It is as important as the ministry to the adults. However, if you have the open door, you work there; but if you are not faithful, don't expect God to promote you.

If you have opportunity to be on the staff of a ministry, remember that you are under the authority of the Pastor, and you should be loyal to him or her. Don't just take the position to get where you are going. Serve there faithfully and do what you are asked to do.

Some people are called to work under another authority, and don't ever realize it. While they are with a successful ministry, everything they do is blessed and prosperous. But after a period of time, they think they would do better on their own. So they leave, but never achieve the same level of success that they had while under the authority of the previous ministry.

Most of the time that indicates a missed calling. Make sure God is leading you to change positions. You can do much more for God in unity. Find your place and stay in it. Don't misunderstand me; God does lead people out. But make sure it's time, and go with the blessings of that ministry. Leaving in strife hurts everyone, but mostly you.

I remember early in my ministry, a tent evangelist asked me if I would be his song leader. I had never done that before and I told him so, but he said, "you can learn." I took the position of directing the singing, and learned to do a good job. Little did I know that the position also meant driving the truck and helping to set up the tent. But I did not move out of my authority; I knew my position. I served him faithfully and made sure all of his personal needs were met. I worked diligently around the tent keeping things in order as if everything was mine.

Yes, I cared that much. It was not something I was enduring until I was allowed to preach. Oh yes, I wanted to preach. I worked hard at my position though, and loved it. I did not have the attitude, "Boy, I just can't wait until I don't have to do this anymore, and I can get into my own ministry." I knew it was an open door. I loved and trusted the evangelist as a man of God. I was not there for a salary; I was there to serve and do what I could faithfully. It was a pleasure because I did it as unto the Lord.

I remember when he asked me to preach in one of the evening services, because he could not be there. I was so excited to have such an opportunity, and the first thing I did was give my thanks to him for letting me speak in his absence. I knew the congregation was not mine, so I

Faith is Love's Confidence

did my best and did not step out of my authority. God honored what I did, and there were many other times when I received the opportunity to minister for him.

I remained faithful until God showed me the time to go on my own. When I did, I went with his blessings--plus he helped me by giving me equipment to get started in my own tent ministry.

If you are a Spirit-filled believer, don't be fickle. Don't hang around those who are giving out bad reports. Remain loyal to the Word and to your spiritual leader. Don't be moved by the decision your friends in the church make; they may be wrong. Pray for the Pastor if he is wrong, but don't leave. The only way to see change wrought is to stay and see your prayer come to pass. Give God a chance to bring His Word to pass. We need unity in the body of Christ, working together, not everyone just doing his own thing.

In Numbers, chapter 13, you can read where ten of the spies were not loyal to God nor Moses. When they saw the giants, they began to complain and said, *We are but grasshoppers in their sight.*

Joshua and Caleb were loyal and faithful, not fickle. They kept their profession of faith. Yes, they saw giants, but they said, *We are able to possess the land, they are meat for us.* They came back and gave a good report. Don't be up one day and down the other, ready to hold up the Pastor today, and then changing your mind tomorrow. If you will support your Pastor, stay loyal to the work of God, and give good reports, we will win the world together. The world will see Christ in us and desire what we have.

The Power Of God's Character

> *Let us hold fast the profession of our faith without wavering; (for he is faithful that promised.)* (Hebrews 10:23)

If you are not faithful on your job in following instructions and doing what you are asked to do by your employer, how can you expect a raise, a better position, or another job? Your attitude must be right. If you are a complainer, God cannot do for you what He has promised. The word "complain" means "to find fault, to make accusations, to express pain or displeasure." A child of the King will be an example of the believer. He will demonstrate the love of God by remining faithful. He will not complain, find fault, or make accusations.

I was privileged to go to Seoul, Korea and spend quality time with Paul Yonggi Cho, the Pastor of the world's largest church. What impressed me the most was the faithfulness of the people to the church and Pastor. The church employees and Pastor had rigid schedules, but none of them complained. They rejoiced in having the opportunity to work for God and serve in the kingdom. Isaiah says,

> *If ye be willing and obedient, ye shall eat the good of the land.* (Isaiah 1:19)

From this you can see that faithfulness is a major part of God's character. What you do for Him must be done with a willing heart and in obedience to those in authority. If you can't follow instructions from God's Word, His leaders, and your employers, you will not eat of the good of the land; you will not be endowed with supernatural gifts of God.

It is important, when you are working for someone else, to look out for their interest. Yes, you have to protect yourself, but the point here is that you have been entrusted with a task. If you are thinking only of what good there is in it for you and don't do everything you know to do, you have no other reward.

And if ye have not been faithful in that which is another man's, who shall give you that which is your own? (Luke 16:12)

Someone once said to me, "You can always tell a man's character by what he does when no one is watching."

When I am doing something for someone else, I do it as if I was doing it for myself. I want my employees to do a good job for me, so I set the example for them. Make that quality decision today to be faithful to God.

Chapter 9

MEEKNESS IS LOVE'S HUMILITY

After reading the prior chapters, you can see the importance of the character of God and how it produces God's power. You must produce today what some have said only happened in the "good ole days." Hebrews 13:8 says, *Jesus Christ the same yesterday, and today, and forever.* The same things Jesus did, you can do today. Miracles are not over. As you reveal Christ, not only in power and conduct, the door will be open to share with others what God has done for you, and what He will do for them. The world is troubled; they need help, and you must help them.

First, you must share. Be different by the life you live, not by some strange actions or doctrine. It's my desire that people would see me as they see Christ.

You don't just put on a front or act a certain way; you actually bring your emotions under control to your spirit. As Christ flows freely through you, you become a spirit-controlled person. Adam was, before he fell in the garden.

I'm reminded of what Jesus said in Matthew 11:28-30.

28 Come unto me, all ye that labour and are heavy laden, and I will give you rest.

29 Take my yoke upon you, and learn of me; for I am meek and lowly in heart: and ye shall find rest unto your souls.

30 For my yoke is easy, and my burden is light.
(Matthew 11:28)

Jesus was meek, but He was also a very aggressive person. He came to do His Father's will. Jesus came to people to help them find rest, and to relieve them of yokes of bondage. Those who seek to develop meekness into their character have opportunity to overcome. Meekness actually means gentle, humble, or balanced. You could say that meek people are balanced in all areas, with an attitude of meekness.

The Webster dictionary definition for meekness is "not inclined to anger or resentment, not boastful." Pride would be the reciprocal of meekness. God desires for you to walk in your righteousness, have self-worth, a high self-esteem. When God blesses you financially or uses you to any degree, you should continue to walk in humility, realizing that there is no cause to be inflated with pride and become boastful, because the good things that are taking place in your life are from the Lord.

According as it is written, He that glorieth, let him glory in the Lord. (1st Corinthians 1:31)

God should get all glory for the things that are accomplished in your life, and when you are used of God in any capacity to help someone else. Stay humble before the Lord. I am the same meek person that I was when I ministered to very small audiences. I am the same person I was when Sharon and I had such limited income that we couldn't even afford a motel room. Prosperity has not changed me. God is my source. I am humble and not filled with pride. I know from where my help and strength comes.

Don't get puffed up. Proverbs tells us this.

18 Pride goeth before destruction, and an haughty spirit before a fall.

19 Better it is to be of an humble spirit with the lowly, than to divide the spoil with the proud. (proverbs 16:18-19)

I have always known that my gift will make room for me and bring me before great men, as promised in Proverbs 18:16.

You do not have to brag or boast of your talents. If you will use them for the glory of God, you will be lifted by the Spirit of God to the place of favor.

6 ...Wherefore he saith, God resisteth the proud, but giveth grace unto the humble.

10 Humble yourselves in the sight of the Lord, and he shall lift you up. (James 4:6,10)

Jesus said, as you humble yourself unto the Lord, He gives you favor. I believe that favor is with both God and man. What God gives you when He exalts you, no man can take away. So if you lift yourself up with pride, you will be brought down. Resist pride, resist the devil, and he will flee from you.

5 Likewise, ye younger, submit yourselves unto the elder. Yea, all of you be subject one to another, and be clothed with humility: for God resisteth the proud, and giveth grace to the humble.

6 Humble yourselves therefore under the mighty hand of God, that he may exalt you in due time. (1st Peter 5:5-6)

There are times when people are used of God, and when they see what God has done through them, they no longer want to submit to authority.

Why?

Because they let pride get in. Peter said to be clothed with humility; don't get your eyes on yourself. Remember, it's God at work in you. The more you keep this in your thinking and actions, the more blessings and favor will come to you. That's the Word of God. You may be working in a position in the church or ministry, and you are called to a higher calling. Stay humble in the sight of the Lord, and He will exalt you when it is time. He will promote you. When He promotes you and gives you a place, you can stay there, because you have not used worldly tactics to get there.

You have seen some people who believe humility is not standing up for themselves, allowing others to take advantage of them. You do not see any example of this in the scriptures. Matthew 5:39 says,

Meekness is Love's Humility

But I say unto you, That ye resist not evil: but whosoever shall smite thee on thy right cheek, turn to him the other also. (Matthew 5:39)

Many have taken this scripture out of context and said you are to take anything people do to you. That's not what Jesus is saying here. He is saying not to get in strife with them, and don't use the same tactics they use.

Romans 12:14 gives the same thought as Matthew 5:39.

Bless them which persecute you: bless, and curse not. (Romans 12:14)

Paul is saying not to retaliate. Do more than what is required. Be kind, even though they are not. Just because they have allowed themselves to be used of the devil, you don't have to. In other words, if omeone has done you wrong, don't sit around and meditate on the wrong they have done and think of how you can get even. Let them do what they do, and you go about your business, as if they are not saying or doing anything. Turn the other cheek, and keep your mind right. Say in your heart, "You're not hurting me. You can't. You are hurting yourself."

Pray for them.

17 Recompense to no man evil for evil. Provide things honest in the sight of all men.

18 If it be possible, as much as lieth in you, live peaceably with all men.

19 Dearly beloved, avenge not yourselves, but rather give place unto wrath: for it it written, Vengeance is mine; I will repay, saith the Lord.

The Power Of God's Character

20 Therefore if thine enemy hunger, feed him; if he thirst, give him drink: for in so doing thou shalt heap coals of fire on his head.

21 Be not overcome of evil, but overcome evil with good. (Romans 12:17-21)

When meekness is working in you, you will put God's Word into action and do what you know to do. Your emotions may be screaming out for you to retaliate, but that's not the time to listen or be moved by your emotions. Allow your spirit to control your emotions. It never seems easy in the beginning, but as you become more and more Spirit-led, your emotions will have less effect on your decisions.

People have lost jobs, Pastors have left churches, and friendships have been broken because rash emotional decisions have been made, rather than people being humble or meek. **Hear** what the Spirit of God is saying.

If you have to suffer the wrong sometimes, do so; God will always bring out the truth. For so long, the body of Christ has reacted to situations emotionally, rather than by the Spirit. When there is a heated argument, both people lose. The one who "wins" feels as if he is in the superior position and has no respect for the loser. The one who "loses" feels put down by the verbal lashing, and consequently has no respect for the winner.

In reality, neither has won, nor truly accomplished anything. Only separation has occurred.

Do what the scriptures say and overcome evil with good. Don't fall into Satan's trap of argument and strife. Do good, instead of trading insults. Be kind to the person who demeans you. By doing so, you heap coals of fire on his head. That wouldn't be an intended result of being meek, but as a result of the invocation of spiritual law.

I have always enjoyed reading the fifth, sixth, and seventh chapters of Matthew. These three chapters are commonly labeled the "Sermon on the Mount," yet they are so much more. They sum up in a nutshell the doctrines of Jesus. By meditating on them for several years, I have been helped tremendously in the areas of overcoming and meekness.

One verse that really stands out to me is Matthew 6:12, *And forgive us our debts, as we forgive our debtors.* I look at others and try to understand why they act the way they do. This helps me to treat them as I would like to be treated. I've found out that if a person gives unselfishly, it will be returned to him good measure, pressed down, shaken together, and running over. Remember this: if you want goodness and kindness to come to you, it must first be given by you.

A fool is quick-tempered; a wise man stays cool when insulted. (Proverbs 12:16 Living)

Love and meekness forget mistakes. If you insult, it parts the best of friends.

It is better to be slow-tempered than famous. (Proverbs 16:32 Living)

A lack of understanding about disagreement is another thing I have noticed among believers. I see it this way: if you don't agree with someone, you don't have to be disagreeable. Do all you can to keep the unity of the faith. Some people have personalities that are not necessarily the type you care to be around, but this is where you should make allowances for people. Don't try to change them; accept them and love them. Do what you know to do and let God bring change. There's so much you can accomplish, if you will make allowances for other people.

2 Living as becomes you--with complete lowliness of mind (humility) and meekness, (unselfishness, gentleness, mildness), with patience, bearing with one another and making allowances because you love one another.

3 Be eager and strive earnestly to guard and keep the harmony and oneness of [produced by] the Spirit in the binding power of peace. (Ephesians 4:2-3 Amp.)

Now let's talk about someone who falls into sin. I am not saying to condone their sin when they have missed the mark, but as the apostle Paul said, "consider yourself." Christians have tended to bury their wounded rather than making allowances for them. I long to see the body as one, and not be individually set up as judges, but as sons of God, loving everyone--even those who have fallen into Satan's snares.

Brethren, if a man be overtaken in a fault, ye which are spiritual, restore such a one in the spirit of meekness; considering thyself, lest thou also be tempted. (Galatians 6:1)

You help restore him to his place in Christ and grace. Don't exalt yourself as someone above the same problem. Show mercy and love. Don't beat a fallen brother.

Time is short. I desire to see Jesus, and I believe He's coming soon. I'll be glad when we no longer have to fight the fight of faith. But until this life is over, I will do all in my power to keep the unity of the faith. We work in this life for the promise, the hope of our new home. I try always to keep that hope in mind. Even when I've been harassed by people and when I've been misunderstood; even when they choose to stop supporting my ministry and leave my church, I realize I can't take it personally. Instead, I look to Jesus, the author and finisher of my faith, and love them the same.

You may get hurt at times by what people say and do, but the secret is to not let those hurt feelings control you. Make allowances for people. I'm not saying to condone wrong, but try to understand them and go on. Let's run this race with patience, love, and kindness, and be excited about God, and the opportunity we have to minister His life to others.

Chapter 10

TEMPERANCE IS LOVE'S VICTORY

I believe we can live a victorious life all the time. The key to walking in victory is having control. A better way to say it is that you cannot be spirit-controlled until you have self-control.

Temperance means to have self-control and to be moderate in the indulgence of appetite. Webster's dictionary defines it this way: "self-restraint in conduct; self-discipline." As you look at the fruit of the spirit, which is love, it is your responsibility to control and discipline yourself in every area of your life so that love will shine through. Conduct yourself in a manner that gives God glory from your life.

Your soul is where you make the decision to walk in victory and fight the good fight of faith, so that is where temperance is exercised. As a matter of fact, it is the same

The Power Of God's Character

in the other seven areas which I have discussed. Your spirit cannot make decisions. Once you are born again, it has God's life, and only agrees with good. It's your responsibility to develop your emotions into the love that is within your recreated spirit. When you have developed joy, peace, longsuffering, gentleness, goodness, faith, meekness, and temperance in your life, it's love at work.

Some people think, because they are born again and Spirit-filled, it's the devil, if they experience a bad emotion. You are a human being. You will always experience different emotions--and if you continue to let the wrong feeling or emotion control you, then the devil gets involved. There again is where self-control comes in. Religious noise will not get the job done.

And my speech and my preaching was not with enticing words of man's wisdom, but in demonstration of the spirit and of power: (1st Corinthians 2:4)

Paul said it so well. He did not use the means of a great orator to sway men, though he was educated enough to do so. He could have played on the emotions of men, but he knew that would not last and cause men to be changed. He said he preached under the anointing and power of the Spirit, and confirmed what he preached with signs following. Paul had the God-kind of character, and lived in the demonstration of it each day. Paul desired for the people to have their faith in God, and to live like God.

Let's continue looking at the word "temperance." Sometimes when I'm teaching on the subject of the fruit of the spirit, I want to start with temperance first. If you can't bring yourself under control to the Spirit, how can

Temperance is Love's Victory

you ever allow the supernatural gifts to flow through you? You become sensitive to the Spirit as you learn self-control. Paul spoke of your body as being the temple of the Holy Ghost.

But I keep under my body, and bring it into subjection: lest that by any means, when I have preached to others, I myself should be a castaway. (1st Corinthians 9:27)

As a New Testament believer, you must bring your body under subjection (control it). You cannot bring your body under control unless you first renew your mind with God's Word. Renewal of your mind is not a one-time occurrence, it is a daily process.

There is no intention here of bringing condemnation to you, but of opening your eyes to the importance of being a doer of God's Word, even in your body.

Many times, at 5:30 a.m. my body does not want to get up to pray; or my body does not want to be still for several hours when I plan to study the Word. I must have my mind renewed, or my body will win.

My spirit has no decision in the situation. It's all my will.

Many people have good intentions. They set their alarm early enough to pray and meditate in God's Word, but when the alarm goes off, their body says, "Hit the snooze button!"--and they do. When they do that, they don't sleep, because they are lying there in anticipation of it going off again. When it does, they hit it again and again. Then they finally look at the clock, jump up, head to the shower, dress quickly, and put on their tie as they head out the door. They drive fast to get to work on time, and their whole day is filled with frustration.

Why?

Because they let your body rule them. They could have gotten up and prayed all of the time they were hitting the snooze button. Their sleep wasn't that restful during that time anyway.

Some people have told me it takes 45 minutes to an hour for them to get out of bed each day. That same person, when they have to, will get up quickly. They will control their body when they have to. You can all do it all the time.

There will always be those who are late no matter where they go.

Why?

Because they are not controlling their bodies. The degree to which you control your flesh indicates where you are spiritually.

I have heard Norvel Hayes say that our bodies are crazy. I have to agree with him--especially when banana pudding is being served. My body loves banana pudding. I'll have one helping, and my body will tell me to have two more. Well, I have to tell it, "No! Three helpings is too much."

Temperance is moderation in appetite. When we continually renew our mind, we will control our body. The New Testament believer is to be an example. We must protect and keep our bodies.

19 What? Know ye not that your body is the temple of the Holy Ghost which is in you, which ye have of God, and ye are not your own?

20 For ye are bought with a price: therefore glorify God in your body, and in your spirit, which are God's. (1st Corinthians 6:19-20)

Now that you are born again, you no longer live for yourself, but to God. Your body is the dwelling place, the temple of God. You are to glorify God in your body. You do this by bringing it under subjection and not allowing it to rule you.

Everything you do reflects and reveals who is ruling. If you overeat and are overweight, this is not a good testimony of having self-control. When you stand to help someone, I believe you should be an example of what you are talking about. If you desire the nine supernatural gifts, or any one of the five ministry gifts, temperance must be an important part of your life. When people see you, they should see Christ.

I beseech you therefore, Brethren, by the mercies of God, that ye present your bodies a living sacrifice, holy, acceptable unto God, which is your reasonable service. (Romans 12:1)

In the Old Testament, men brought a sacrifice to the altar. God now asks us to bring ourselves. Bring your body to God. Make it a living sacrifice, holy, and acceptable to God. Fill it with light, reckon it dead to sin; now alive unto God. Refuse to defile it. Make it a fit temple or dwelling place for the Holy Spirit. Glorify God in it; keep it in control.

And take heed to yourselves, lest at any time your hearts be overcharged with surfeiting, and drunkenness, and cares of this life, and so that day come upon you unawares. (Luke

21:34)

In this scripture, Jesus puts several things in the same category: surfeiting, drunkenness, and the cares of life. He is saying here that overeating, drunkenness, and worry will have the same effect.

Lay these things aside by the act of your will. Paul is saying that you are the temple of God, and the Spirit of God dwells in you. Therefore, you are to keep your body holy.

I believe God is now bringing more revelation to the body of Christ than at any other time in history. As the light of God continues to come, the body of Christ will walk in self-control. God's character will be at work in it--unity and oneness of purpose, instead of pulling against each other. The body will work together to see the nine spiritual gifts in operation in the lives of all believers. Signs will accompany them, and they will cause millions to accept Jesus Christ into their lives.

> *5 For this reason, make every effort to add to your faith goodness; and to goodness, knowledge;*
>
> *6 and to knowledge, self-control; and to self-control, perseverance; and to perseverance, godliness;*
>
> *7 and to godliness, brotherly kindness; and to brotherly kindness, love.*
>
> *8For if you posses these qualities in increasing measure, they will keep you from being ineffective and unproductive in your knowledge of our Lord Jesus Christ.* (2nd Peter 1:5-8 NIV)

These verses of scripture sum up everything you have been taught in this portion of the book. Now a foundation has been laid to walk in love and to be a genuine twentieth century believer.

You should first of all have these divine qualities at work in your life. Then all the others--such as the nine supernatural gifts and the five ministry gifts--come later.

Chapter 11

THE HOLY SPIRIT

Receiving the Holy Spirit is a separate experience from being born again. Accepting Jesus Christ into your heart is the new life, and the passing away of the old. The Holy Spirit brings the change from the old to the new, and it is eternal.

Therefore if any man be in Christ, he is a new creature: old things are passed away; behold, all things are become new. (2nd Corinthians 5:17)

You are born again by believing on Jesus and confessing him as your Savior.

9 That if thou shalt confess with thy mouth the Lord Jesus, and shalt believe in thine heart that God hath raised him from the dead, thou shalt be saved.

10 For with the heart man believeth unto righteousness; and with the mouth confession is

The Power Of God's Character

made unto salvation. (Romans 10:9-10)

At the new birth, you are saved from spiritual death and made alive to Christ Jesus. You become a child of God, you can have communication with God through prayer, and you will go to heaven. However, there is much more for the New Testament believer. The Holy Spirit is at work in the new birth, **but there is the receiving or being filled with the Holy Spirit** that follows the new birth.

The Holy Spirit gives you more power to overcome the temptations in this life, plus He gives you power to be on the offensive against the devil and for what belongs to you. In other words, some people just hold their ground, but with the Holy Spirit, you are able to make progress and possess what the Word of God says you can possess.

> *But ye shall receive power, after that the Holy Ghost is come upon you: and ye shall be witnesses unto me both in Jerusalem, and in all Judea, and in Samaria, and unto the uttermost part of the earth.* (Acts 1:8)

You receive power *after that the Holy Ghost is come upon you.* The word "power" here comes from the Greek word "dunamis," which means "miraculous power: ability, abundance, strength." This is all contained in the Holy Ghost, and is available for every born again child of God.

> *If ye then, being evil, know how to give good gifts unto your children; how much more shall your heavenly Father give the Holy Spirit to them that ask him?* (Luke 11:13)

Receiving the Holy Spirit will give you the strength and power to do things that you could not do without it. The Holy Spirit is necessary for every born again child of God.

And I will ask the Father, and He will give you another Comforter (Counselor, Helper, Intercessor, Advocate, Strengthener and Standby) that He may remain with you forever. (John 14:16 Amp.)

Why would any Christian not want this extra help of the Holy Ghost? Some of the reasons would be that they do not know it's for them, or they have been told by someone that it's not for people today. I'm reminded of a story of a young man walking down the street with a book under his arm. Someone approached him and said, "Say, young man, what is that dilapidated book under your arm"?

"Oh, that's my Bible".

"Why is it so torn up and thin?"

"Well, at the church I attend, my pastor is always telling me that this part of the Bible, and that part of the Bible is not for us today. And I figure if it isn't for me today, I might as well tear out that part of it. So you can see that this is all I have left".

Many Christians have that attitude about the Word of God. They have been told it's not for today, and that has caused them to go without the help of the Holy Spirit.

My people are destroyed for lack of knowledge: (Hosea 4:6)

Many people really don't know what is available to them from God, because their leaders have not told them.

You must ask and seek Him through the Word and in prayer. There is help from the Holy Spirit, if you desire for Him to come into your life. He will be a comfort in the time of need, He will counsel you, He will help you in intercession, He will give you extra strength, and He will stand by you when you feel as if you have no one else.

Even the Spirit of truth; whom the world cannot receive, because it seeth him not, neither knoweth him: but ye know him; for he dwelleth with you, and shall be in you. (John 14:16)

Here again, He is saying the Holy Spirit is for the believer, the person who is born again. If you fit into this category, then you are a candidate to receive the Holy Spirit. When you are born again, He is with you; after you receive the Holy Spirit, He shall be in you with miraculous power to do the works of God, to live the life of freedom, and to keep Satan under your feet. You'll have more than enough power to meet any need you will have or face in this life.

When a person receives the Holy Spirit, according to the scriptures, they will speak in tongues. You do not seek tongues, you ask for the Holy Spirit, and your prayer language comes with the Holy Spirit.

When you are going to purchase a pair of lace-up shoes, the shoes have tongues in them. You didn't go buy a pair of tongues, did you? They were an important part of the shoes, and they came with them. In the same way, tongues is a part of the Holy Spirit; the initial outward evidence.

Before I show you scriptural truth which proves that speaking in tongues is for the Spirit-filled believer, I want

The Holy Spirit

you to look at some arguments people have used in saying they believe speaking in tongues has ceased.

> *8 Charity never faileth: but whether there be prophecies, they shall fail;* **whether there be tongues, they shall cease**; *whether there be knowledge, it shall vanish away.*
>
> *9 For we know in part, and we prophesy in part.*
>
> *10 But when that which is perfect is come, then that which is in part shall be done away.*
>
> *11 When I was a child, I spake as a child, I understood as a child, I thought as a child: but when I became a man, I put away childish things.*
>
> *12 For now we see through a glass, darkly; but then face to face: now I know in part; but then shall I know even as as I am known.* (1st Corinthians 13:8-12)

The people who use these verses of scripture to support their belief that tongues is not for today have overlooked verse eight. There is more mentioned here than tongues. He said prophecies would fail and knowledge would vanish. You can see that this is not true. Daniel 12:4 says that knowledge will increase in the last day. Prophecies have not failed, knowledge has not vanished; **neither has tongues ceased.**

It is very evident that knowledge has increased, and prophecies are still coming to pass. The gospel is being preached more that ever before. The cassette recorder, television, radio, and the printed Word are taking the message of Jesus to all the world. All this is prophecy coming to pass. God gave us the knowledge to do it.

These are tools that we are using to reach the world.

And he said unto them, Go ye into all the world, and preach the gospel to every creature. (Mark 16:15)

Isaiah prophesied that in the last days God's Spirit would be poured out upon all flesh. We are now seeing the fulfillment of that prophecy. We are seeing a greater outpouring of God's Spirit than ever before. So prophecy has not ceased.

For we know in part, and we prophesy in part. (1st Corinthians 13:9)

We don't know all things. Now, we do have knowledge and prophecy, which gives us a part.

For now we see through a glass darkly: but then face to face: now I know in part; but then shall I know even as also I am known. (1st Corinthians 13:12)

When we get to heaven there will be no need of any gift. It will be unveiled there and we will know as we are known. So if you are going to take the part out of this passage of scripture where Paul said, *whether there be tongues, they shall cease*, you will have to eliminate prophecy and knowledge.

When you look at it in the context in which it was given, you can understand that he is not dealing with speaking in tongues as a prayer language. He is speaking of the time when we are in heaven. There in heaven, we will have no need for tongues, prophecy, or knowledge. We will know all things.

The Holy Spirit

Another area of misunderstanding is found in First Corinthians Twelve. I meditated in this chapter to see what Paul was talking about. In verse 27 he said there are some particular members of the body he wanted you to know about. Verse 28 says that God has set in the church- -the body--Apostles, Prophets, Teachers, miracles, and then gifts of healings. This last is the ministry of the Evangelist. Helps and government are in the ministry of the Pastor. God places a Pastor. He is to oversee the local church, and all the helps involved in the ministry come under his supervision.

When Paul speaks of diversities of tongues, he is still talking about ministry, not receiving the Holy Spirit, or whether all will speak in tongues when they receive the Holy Spirit. He is actually talking about the ministry of diversities of tongues.

In verse 29, Paul asks the question, *are all Apostles? No.* He went on to ask also, *Are all prophets? No.* He went on to ask also, *Are all prophets? No. Are all teachers? No. Do all speak in tongues? Do all interpret?*

He is asking if all logically have a public ministry of delivering a message in tongues. That must be what he's saying, because the next thing he asks is, *do all interpret?* There cannot be an interpretation unless there is first a message in tongues.

There is nothing implied here about receiving the Holy Ghost and speaking with tongues. In verse 31 he says to covet the best gifts, and tongues is your prayer language. It comes with the baptism of the Holy Spirit; but diversities of tongues is a gift separate from speaking in tongues. He is dealing with ministry here; not with being filled with the Holy Spirit.

I believe all scripture is given by inspiration to teach the things of God. I would not be guilty of taking scripture out of context to prove a point. I meditate in the Word to see what is really being said.

A carnal mind cannot understand the things of God; it takes a spiritual mind to have revelation knowledge. It's important that you spend time in prayer, and meditate in the Word. Don't just take the word of someone else, or that of a commentary, to put you in one accord with the Spirit of God. If someone is saying something that is not in line with what the Word is really saying, then you'll know it by the Spirit. God will reveal His Word to you to give you clear understanding, and to know without a shadow of a doubt what His Word is saying in each setting.

Speaking in tongues is the initial outward manifestation of the Holy Spirit. You will speak in tongues when you receive the Holy Spirit.

*And they were all filled with the Holy Ghost, **and began to speak with other tongues**, as the Spirit gave them utterance.* (Acts 2:4)

You can see in this scripture that all of those in the upper room received the Holy Ghost. They spoke with tongues as the Spirit gave them utterance. The people used their vocal cords, their tongues, their lips; they did the speaking. God did not make them receive; He responded to their act of faith (speaking) with the utterance. They were waiting for the promise.

Some people say, "If He wants me to have it, then He will give it to me".

The Holy Spirit

Well, He won't knock you unconscious to make you speak in tongues.

Remember, God has given you a will; you can choose to follow Him closely, or at a distance. God does not force you to do anything. You must make the effort to speak, if you desire the Holy Spirit. When you accepted Jesus Christ as your savior and Lord, He did not make you receive Him; you had to do it by faith. You used your vocal cords, your lips; you made that confession of your own free will.

Receiving the Holy Spirit is no different; it's by faith. When they were in the upper room, they were not there waiting until they were all in one accord. They went there in one accord waiting for the promise, and it came on the day of Pentecost. The Holy Spirit was given on that day.

You do not have to tarry long hours, days, weeks, months, or even years to receive. All you have to do is ask in faith, and He will give it to you.

Remember, God knows your heart. If you're not sincere in your request, He's not going to give you something that you really don't want.

Some people say, "I got down on my knees, and nothing happened."

Most people in this case were not really expecting the experience, because of either fear or wrong teaching.

Then there is the extreme which I have already mentioned. Some think God will knock them out, and when they revive, they will be speaking in tongues.

God does everything in order. There is nothing to be afraid of, as He only gives His children good gifts.

38 Then Peter said unto them, Repent, and be baptized every one of you in the name of Jesus Christ for the remission of sins, and ye shall receive the gift of the Holy Ghost.

39 For the promise is unto you, and to your children, and to all that are afar off, even as many as the Lord our God shall call. (Acts 2:38-39)

Peter gave very good instructions. He said repent, then you will receive. Notice that he said this promise is to you and to your children and to them that are afar off. That sentence is straightforward, and doesn't lend itself to misunderstanding. The Holy Spirit is for everyone. It has not been done away with. If you have not received, make yourself available, and let the Holy Spirit come in.

The day of Pentecost is the first example of speaking in tongues. However, we can see evidence in the New Testament of other people receiving the Holy Spirit after Pentecost.

12 But when they believed Philip preaching the things concerning the kingdom of God, and the name of Jesus Christ, they were baptized, both men and women.

13 Then Simon himself believed also; and when he was baptized, he continued with Philip, and wondered, beholding the miracles and signs which ere done.

14 Now when the apostles which were at Jerusalem heard that Samaria had received the word of God, they went unto them Peter and John:

15 Who, when they were come down, prayed for them, that they might receive the Holy Ghost:

16 (For as yet he was fallen upon none of them: only they were baptized in the name of the Lord Jesus.)

17 Then laid they their hands on them, and they received the Holy Ghost.

18 And when Simon saw that through laying on of the apostles' hands the Holy Ghost was given, he offered them money,

19 Saying, Give me also this power, that on whomsoever I lay hands, he may receive the Holy Ghost. (Acts 8:12-19)

Here is another occasion where the Holy Ghost was given. The scripture does not say that they spoke in tongues. However, there was physical evidence or manifestation, because Simon was offering money to have the gift. Logically, this gift was speaking in tongues.

In Acts chapter nine, Paul was born again. God sent Ananias to Paul to lay hands on him. In verse seventeen, he said to Paul, ...*receive thy sight, and be filled with the Holy Ghost.* Here it does not say that Paul spoke in tongues, but in First Corinthians 14:18 Paul said, *"I thank my God, I speak with tongues more than ye all."*

Paul did speak with tongues, and, of course, this was after the outpouring on the day of Pentecost. In acts, chapter ten, Peter received a mandate from God to go to the house of Cornelius. While he was preaching, the Holy Ghost fell on them.

> *44 While Peter yet spake these words, the Holy Ghost fell on all them which heard the word.*
>
> *45 And they of the circumcision which believed were astonished, as many as came with Peter, because that on the Gentiles also was poured out the gift of the Holy Ghost.*
>
> *46 For they heard them speak with tongues, and magnify God.* (Acts 10:44-46)

You will notice that they did speak with tongues. This was ten years after Pentecost.

Once again, the Holy Spirit was given to a group of people at Ephesus, this time twenty years after Pentecost. In Acts 19:1-6, Paul learned they had been baptized unto John's baptism. Verse five says Paul then baptized them in the name of the Lord Jesus. After that, in verse six, he laid his hands on them and the Holy Ghost came upon them, and they spoke with tongues.

> *2 For he that speaketh in an unknown tongue speaketh not unto men, but unto God: for no man understandeth him; howbeit in the spirit he speaketh mysteries.*
>
> *4 He that speaketh in an unknown tongue edifieth himself; but he that prophesieth edifieth the church.* (1st Corinthians 14:2-4)

I want to point out several things to you. **First,** God gives you a language for you to talk to Him. This is private and personal, between you and God.

Second, you can pray with tongues anytime you want to. You do not have to feel a special unction from the Spirit. You speak the English language, and you don't have to feel something in order to speak it. You know how to talk, so you do it at your will. It's the same when you receive the Holy Spirit. You can talk to God any time you want to in your prayer language, at your will.

The people I grew up around did not use their prayer language; they thought they had to have a special feeling or unction to speak with tongues. But it's not true; it's your language that God gave you, and you can talk to Him anytime.

Third, When you pray with tongues, no one understands you. Man is not supposed to; your human spirit is praying to God. You are bypassing your intellect. It is spirit to Spirit, nothing hindering your prayers.

Fourth, when you are praying in tongues, another great advantage is that the devil does not know what is being said. He cannot understand the language of the Spirit.

Fifth, when you pray with tongues, secrets are revealed and made known to you. Revelation is given to you. You can know more about a situation when you pray in tongues. The mysteries will be revealed as your mind becomes quiet, and He begins to speak to you.

Sixth, When you pray with tongues, you are edified or built up. You receive confirmation and instruction from the Holy Spirit.

But ye, beloved, building up yourselves on your most holy faith, praying in the Holy Ghost. (Jude 20)

When Sharon and I hurt so badly, we had no words in English that we could say to God. We didn't understand some of the things that had happened in our family; so we prayed hours with tongues, and the Spirit built us up. He

The Power Of God's Character

gave us joy and victory. Our intellect seemed empty and void; but our spirits knew how to pray, because we had the Holy Spirit. Our spirits were able to commune with God, until we could pray with understanding. I could not have made it through without the Holy Spirit. He prayed through me. I thank God for the Holy Ghost!

26 Likewise the Spirit also helpeth our infirmities; for we know not what we should pray for as we ought: but the Spirit itself maketh intercession for us with groanings which cannot be uttered.

27 And he that searcheth the hearts knoweth what is the mind of the Spirit, because he maketh intercession for the saints according to the will of God. (Romans 8:26-27)

Many times in my life and ministry, I haven't known how to pray. The Spirit has helped me, strengthened me in my weakness, and interceded for me as I prayed with tongues. He knows my heart, and He always prays God's will for me. Don't be robbed of the blessings of God by not using your prayer language. Pray often with tongues.

There are times when God will use you to pray with tongues for others. You may not know how to pray, but God will intercede for you with groanings which cannot be uttered. You will always pray the will of God when you pray with tongues.

14 For if I pray in an unknown tongue, my spirit prayeth but my understanding is unfruitful.

15 What is it then? I will pray with the spirit, and I will pray with the understanding also: I will sing with the spirit, and I will sing with the understanding also. (1st Corinthians 14:14-15)

Paul is saying here, when you pray with tongues, you do not understand what your spirit is praying. What is actually happening as you pray in tongues is that God reveals to you what to do and how to pray. You are given understanding, so Paul says, *I pray in the spirit and then I will pray with my understanding; I will sing in the spirit and then I will sing in understanding.*

Keep in mind, though, that this is done privately. This is not talking about a public gathering. When you pray in a public gathering, you should always pray in your understanding so that those who hear you may also understand.

When you speak in tongues in a public gathering, it should be the gift of tongues with an interpretation. I admonish you to take full advantage of your prayer language; pray without ceasing.

At this point I want to deal with a matter which I believe needs some instruction.

That there should be no schism in the body; but that the members should have the same care one for another. (1st Corinthians 12:25)

In other words, there should be no division among us. Separation has been brought into the midst of the body of Christ, because there have been disagreements and differing opinions. These have caused many to cease loving others in the body.

Unfortunately, in some areas, division and separation have escalated to the point where some no longer recognize those who differ with them doctrinally as part of the family of God. I believe, if a person is born again by having taken Jesus as his Lord and Savior, then he is my brother in Christ. This does not necessarily mean that I have to attend the same church or believe what he believes, but I will welcome him as a member of the body of Christ. I will show him love and kindness, and pray for him.

This is no time to fight against one another or to do things that will cause division. We need to find a point of agreement and work together from there where we can. We need to use our time and energy helping to unify the body, rather than tearing it down.

I believe speaking in tongues is important, and I believe all New Testament believers can and should do so. But if you don't at this point in time, you can when you receive revelation and understanding. If you are truly born again, even if you do not speak in tongues, you are no less accepted as a part of the body of Christ than one who does.

Speaking in tongues does not make me a better person than you by any means; but it certainly makes me better than I was.

First Corinthians 12:14 tells us, *For the body is not one member, but many.*

There are lots of believers in this world, and the way you can strengthen them and begin doing your part in helping to pull them together is to do everything out of love. Every member of the body of Christ should be important to you, because you are a part of the same body. It is your responsibility to grow in your Christian walk

The Holy Spirit

with God. As you do, you should walk in the light which you have received.

If the kind of teaching which promotes growth is not being given in the church where you attend, then go where the uncompromised, full-gospel truth is being taught. I am not saying for you to go from church to church. I am saying, though, if the church you are worshipping at now does not teach the uncompromised Word, then find one that does, and stay put.

If you speak in tongues and believe in the spiritual gifts, but the church you attend does not, you will have difficulty growing into a mature Christian. You will reap only frustration, bitterness, and strife, if you stay there and try to change it.

Why is that?

The pastor of that church is in authority there. If you have gone to him and told him of your experience, but he does not receive it, you will be out of order if you contest his authority by attempting to spread there what you have received elsewhere. You will cause confusion--and God is not the author of confusion. God does not split churches, so don't cause problems for yourself and the pastor by teaching things which he does not approve of.

Therefore leaving the principles of the doctrine of Christ, let us go on unto perfection: not laying again the foundation of repentance from dead works, and of faith toward God. (Hebrews 6:1)

The word "perfection" here comes from the Greek word "telelotes" which means "a completer, consummator, finisher." The writer of Hebrews is encouraging you to be a completer or finisher. Don't stay in the same place spiritually; grow up. Don't limit yourself just because those you associate with have only grown to a certain point. Step out... grow up... move out with love.

Cease, my son, to hear the instruction that causeth to err from the words of knowledge. (Proverbs 19:27)

In other words, don't listen to instruction that is against revelation knowledge which you already have. You shouldn't expose yourself to teaching that contradicts what has already been given to you, such as the theory that speaking in tongues is not for today, or that the gifts of the Spirit have been done away with.

So then faith cometh by hearing, and hearing by the word of God. (Romans 10:17)

Your faith is built by hearing and understanding the Word. If God is leading you into greater revelation knowledge, such as is being given in this book, make the decision to develop into a mature Christian. Be a finisher, a completer, of what you have begun.

If you have been attending two churches, you cannot be faithful to either one. I understand that you may start out that way in order to make sure of your direction, but don't do it permanently. You must make a choice. You cannot have two husbands or two wives; neither can you have two churches. You need one church and one pastor to help guide and shape you into the mature Christian that God desires you to be.

The baptism of the Holy Spirit is vital to this, and if you have not received it, **STOP**; lay this book down and ask for the infilling of the Holy Spirit. He will come in and abide with you forever.

Chapter 12

CONCERNING GIFTS

When I was a teenager, the healing revival was in full swing. There were many great men of God on the scene who had God's power operating in their lives. Mighty miracles were performed through their ministries which stirred entire cities. Hundreds and thousands would get saved in one service. There was evidence that the supernatural power of God was at work in and through their lives.

Because of this, many people put their eyes and faith on the man, and did very little studying for themselves--which left room for error. In some cases, since these men had very powerful preaching ministries (at this time teachers were not very exciting), people would go where the "action" was. Some of the preaching was good; some was not.

There were many miracles and things people could "see", so they were moved by their emotions. Many of

The Power Of God's Character

them put their trust in the man and went from meeting to meeting following him, because they felt helpless on their own. Their faith was such that, if they could only get to this man of God, they would be healed. It seemed as if they had more faith in his touch than in God's power to heal.

People would not even take their Bibles to church in many of the places. The meetings were good though, and the gifts of the Spirit did operate through these great men. But the people attending these meetings lived mostly in the valley, up periodically, but mostly down. The majority of their lives were like a roller coaster. While in church, in the presence of the man of God, they would feel great, because they believed he knew God and was on a level with Him--a level that they could never attain. They did not know how to live in victory; therefore, their victory came at the next crusade.

This is not to insult or put down these times, as thousands were saved and healed, and there were demonstrations of God's power. Thank God for these times!

But during this time, most people made no effort to be used of God. They thought the gifts of the Spirit were only for those in the ministry. They believed that they could never have this power, because they were never good enough. Some of the men and women of God depended heavily upon the supernatural gifts to operate in the services, in order for them to be thought of as successful. If in any service there was not a mighty demonstration of the gifts, they were greatly disappointed, and sometimes even discouraged.

In some of the men of God, there was also a lack of knowing and understanding their righteousness. This

Concerning Gifts

caused them to feel inferior in their daily lives. When they were under the anointing and ministering by the gifts of the Spirit though, they were very bold. They seemingly would exercise their authority only when special anointings were upon them. Because of this, some of them could not handle and deal with the pressure Satan brought against them. It seemed as if they had more faith in God's gift than in His Word.

Then came the Charismatic Movement. Many people in this movement felt they did not need anyone to teach them, because they were baptized in the Holy Spirit. This caused a great deal of confusion, as there was little or no teaching being brought forth on what to do with this newly acquired power. Soon though, it produced a new group of people who began to study the Word. This began the Word Movement. The Word began to be taught everywhere with such power and might. It was like a breath of fresh air. This change was so influential that preaching almost became obsolete. People began to see how they had the faith of God (Mark 11:22) and they could believe God for themselves.

People began to understand Second Timothy 1:7, *For God hath not given us the spirit of fear; but of power, and of love, and of a sound mind.* Believers were stronger than ever before because of the Word.

As this took place, more emphasis was put on the much needed subject of righteousness. This brought to people the revelation that they were the very righteousness of God in Christ Jesus. This in turn caused the feelings of inferiority that Christianity had embraced for so long to begin to leave.

The Power Of God's Character

Throughout the Healing Movement, Charismatic Movement, and Word Movement, there was a decline of the operation of some of the nine gifts of the Spirit, and this caused a great void. What is happening now, though, is that there is a balance in the body of Christ. There is Word teaching and instruction. Also, believers are learning how to flow with the Spirit. I believe at this time people will be used in a greater way than at any other time, because of the foundation of God's Word.

I believe you must desire spiritual gifts, make yourself available to God, be sensitive to Him--and you will be used of Him. You will see greater results than you have seen at any other time in your life because of the great amount of intercession and compassion that now is in the body of Christ.

I want you to take a close look at First Corinthians, chapters twelve, thirteen, and fourteen. All of these chapters are actually one subject. Paul is writing there about the gifts of the Spirit coupled with love.

In chapter twelve, he describes the nine gifts of the Spirit and their importance. He also expounds on the body of Christ, emphasizing how important each member of the body is to the other. In addition, he talks some about the special ministries.

But covet earnestly the best gifts: and yet shew I unto you a more excellent way. (1st Corinthians 12:31)

Paul is telling us that he would show us something more important than the gifts of the Spirit and the ministry gifts. He does not say, or even imply, that either of these are to be done away with, or to not be a part of the

New Testament Church. He is saying that love is the most important thing in your life. Actually, chapter thirteen, verse one should be part of chapter twelve.

Though I speak with the tongues of men and of angels, and have not charity, I am become as sounding brass, or a tinkling cymbal. (1st Corinthians 13:1)

Paul's train of thought does not change. He says in this verse that any of the gifts which are manifested without love are nothing more than a religious noise.

You can now see why I dedicated the first part of this book to the fruit of the Spirit, because the fruit must be love at work in all areas of your life.

In chapter thirteen, verse thirteen, Paul says that the greatest characteristic is love.

And now abideth faith, hope, charity, these three; but the greatest of these is charity. (1st Corinthians 13:13)

You notice that he is staying on the same subject. Also, chapter fourteen, verse one is actually a continuation of chapter thirteen.

What does Paul say is in verse one?

He says to follow after love first--seek love, and desire spiritual gifts. In chapter fourteen, verse twelve, he says, if you desire spiritual gifts, ask for the ones that will help edify and encourage the body of Christ. Asking God for spiritual gifts with this attitude is real love, because you are putting others before yourself.

The gifts of the Spirit are given to edify the body of Christ and make it stronger. The gifts are not given to make a great show of power, but instead, to bring forth unity and healing--thus meeting needs in the body.

Paul says in First Corinthians 12:1-3 that he does not want any misunderstanding about the spiritual gifts. Some at the church of Corinth were trying to imitate the spiritual gifts: and in doing so would curse Christ, because they were not born again. It was causing confusion, so Paul told them that no one could curse Christ, if he was speaking by the anointing and power of the Holy Spirit. Neither can anyone call Jesus his Lord and operate in the gifts of the Spirit, except by the Holy Ghost.

In First Corinthians 12:31 he says, *"Covet earnestly the best gifts".*

What are the best gifts? They are the ones needed most at a particular time.

God does not just "give" you one of the nine gifts of the Spirit and say, "This is your gift; use it anytime you want to." Instead, He gives you the Holy Spirit, and as the Holy Spirit wills, the gifts will be manifested to meet the need (1st Corinthians 12:1).

I will discuss in later chapters how the five ministry gifts have certain of the nine spiritual gifts to accompany them. You cannot scripturally claim any particular gift of the Spirit, even though you may have one or more of them operating in your life on a regular basis. The nine spiritual gifts are special endowments of supernatural power, rather than the normal power given to the Spirit-filled believer. This supernatural power is given for a specific time and purpose. The gifts of the Spirit are not restricted to those that are in the ministry, but are given for every Spirit-filled believer.

4 Now there are diversities of gifts, but the same Spirit.

5 And there are differences of administrations, but the same Lord. (1st Corinthians 12:4-5)

The word "differences" and "diversities" from these two verses are from the same Greek word "diairesis," which means "variety." There is a variety of gifts, but it is the same Holy Spirit that produces them. According to verse five, there is a variety of ministry gifts, but the same Spirit calls and anoints various ones to minister in the specific areas to which they are called.

And there are diversities of operations, but it is the same God which worketh all in all. (1st Corinthians 12:6)

There are different gifts which operate in the life of the believer to accomplish or produce what is necessary, but the same Spirit brings it forth. The manifestation of the Spirit is given to profit or to help, and to edify.

But the manifestation of the Spirit is given to every man to profit withal. (1st Corinthians 12:7)

The gifts of the Spirit will always comfort you. They will never confuse, hurt or embarrass you. Anyone who is used by God in the gifts of the Spirit will not be puffed up, use that gift to draw attention to himself, or set himself up above someone else. Instead, he will be humble and understand that it is God's supernatural power at work.

In the first chapter of this book, I talked about the necessity of **prayer and having compassion. This is the number one condition for the gifts of the Spirit**

to be manifested in your life.

Beware of those who supposedly display great gifts, but have no revelation of the Word, as well as those who will not submit themselves to a local church and pastor.

21 Not every one that saith unto me, Lord, Lord, shall enter into the kingdom of heaven; but he that doeth the will of my Father which is in heaven.

22 Many will say to me in that day, Lord Lord, have we not prophesied in thy name? and in thy name have cast out devils? and in thy name done many wonderful works?

23 And then will I profess unto them, I never knew you: depart from me, ye that work iniquity. (Matthew 7:21-23)

Jesus is saying here that some will say "they" have done great miracles. Jesus did not say that they were doing the miracles. "They" were claiming to do the works, but He said, "I have not approved of you".

8 For to one is given by the Spirit the word of wisdom; to another the word of knowledge by the same Spirit;

9 To another faith by the same Spirit; to another the gifts of healing by the same Spirit;

10 To another the working of miracles; to another prophecy; to another discerning of spirits; to another divers kinds of tongues; to another the interpretation of tongues:

11 But all these worketh that one and the selfsame Spirit, dividing to every man severally as

Concerning Gifts

he will. (1st Corinthians 12:8-11)

Paul tells us the Spirit divides the gifts to every believer as the Spirit of God wills to manifest them. This does not mean your will has nothing to do with the gifts operating in you. You must desire them and exercise your faith in that area.

The gifts of the Spirit are divided into three different categories:

1. The revelation gifts:

    a. The word of wisdom:
    this gift reveals or takes a glimpse into the future.

    b. The word of knowledge:
    this gift reveals something in the past or present.

    c. The discerning of spirits:
    this gift gives insight
    into the spiritual world.

All three of these gifts reveal something, and they are all closely associated.

2. The gifts of power:

    a. The gift of faith:
    a special power or ability beyond your own faith.

    b. The gift of working of miracles:

supernatural power that changes things, rather than the normal cause of nature.

c. The gifts of healing:

bring instant healing; total recovery is evident at the instant the gift is manifested.

These three gifts are also very closely associated.

3. **The gifts of inspiration:**

    a. The gift of tongues:

    a supernatural message inspired by God in an unknown tongue.

    b. The interpretation of tongues:

    a supernatural utterance inspired by God to reveal what was said by the unknown tongue.

    c. The gift of prophecy:

    a supernatural utterance inspired by God in a known tongue that edifies, exhorts and comforts.

These three gifts all tie together. But the greatest one of the three is prophecy.

My desire is to define the gifts in such a way that you can understand them, not just from an analytical standpoint, but also from their operation. I want to share with you my experiences with the gifts and show you how to have the same supernatural power of God at work in you.

Chapter 13

THE WORD OF WISDOM

Of the three revelation gifts, the word of wisdom is the greatest. Take notice that it is not the "gift of wisdom." It is a gift of **the word of** wisdom. This gift sees or looks into the future. It does not tell all of the future; but is gives a glimpse or insight on a particular event or situation. It gives you direction, or reveals to you things that are to come.

The word of wisdom can come to you in several ways. The Holy Spirit could show you a vision.

Anytime God reveals something to you by the word of wisdom, it is always to help you. It is never to put fear or frustration upon you; but this is true in all of the nine gifts of the Spirit.

He may tell you something about the future that is not very pleasant. The reason for this would be for you to prepare for this event, or **to go to prayer and change**

The Power Of God's Character

it.

Once I was riding with someone in a van, and all of a sudden I had an impression. I said to the person driving, "slow down!"

Just as he did, another car turned into the street, right in front us. As we drove down just a little bit further, the car which pulled out in front of us was struck. It was a horrible accident. If we had not slowed down, it would have been us.

I did not know that anything was going to happen; I only knew enough to tell him to slow down. It was enough to save us from being hurt, or possibly killed.

In Second Kings 20:1-5, Isaiah the prophet was given a word of wisdom for King Hezekiah. He told him, "Your sickness is unto death. Get your house in order, or you shall die and not live."

Hezekiah believed Isaiah. He said, "Lord, I've tried to please You and obey You in everything I do."

He cried before the Lord, and his cry changed the verdict. It changed the future.

God can help you with your future also, if you will trust Him.

Before Isaiah left the courtyard, another word was given to him for Hezekiah; "Your prayer has been heard, you shall have fifteen more years."

In the book of Genesis is one of the great examples of a man who had the word of wisdom operating in his life. Joseph was only seventeen years old when God began to deal with him in this manner.

The first word of wisdom that he experienced came to him in a dream. He told his dream to his brothers, but they did not understand him.

Later he was sold, taken to Egypt, and put into prison. While he was in prison, there were two men who had dreams; but they were not able to interpret them. One of them was a butler, the other was a baker. They told Joseph their dreams, and by the word of wisdom, he gave them the interpretation. This experience brought Joseph to the King. When he had a dream, Joseph gave the interpretation to the King's two dreams. Because he was able to interpret them, the lives of his family members were saved.

In Isaiah 53, the prophet predicted how Jesus would carry grief, sorrow, and sickness; how the stripes would be placed on His back.

4 Surely he hath borne our griefs, and carried out sorrows: yet we did esteem him stricken, smitten of God, and afflicted.

5 But he was wounded for our transgressions, he was bruised for our iniquities: the chastisement of our peace was upon him; and with his stripes we are healed. (Isaiah 53:4-5)

Joel declared that there would be an outpouring of the Holy Ghost. It took place on the day of Pentecost, and it is still being manifested today.

Moses was given the Ten Commandments.

Daniel interpreted the handwriting on the wall.

Jeremiah, in chapter 31, prophesied of the New Covenant; of how our sins would be forgiven.

Ezekiel, in chapter 36, prophesied that, by the New Birth, our old stony heart would be replaced with a heart of flesh.

Samuel anointed Saul and David to be kings.

All of this was done by the word of wisdom.

Yes, all these men were prophets. The prophet's ministry has the revelation gifts accompanying it in the Old and New Testament, as well as in this present day.

In the Old Testament, the prophets were given a message to warn cities of their evil. Jonah was sent to Ninevah, but he did not want to go. After his detour in the belly of a great fish, he went, and he told them of their future and judgment. They believed him, repented, and changed their situation.

The word of wisdom is always for your good. You may not always like what you hear, but it is given to help you.

Jesus gave the signs of His return in Matthew twenty four. We are presently witnessing what Jesus said would happen. And there are other things yet to take place that He spoke of. This is the word of wisdom revealing the future so that we still know how to live our lives and be prepared for the events that will occur.

Several years ago, I was preaching in Little Rock, Arkansas, under my big tent. During the night, I had a dream of a tornado hitting the small town of Alabama in which I lived at the time. I dreamed that it was coming toward my house. I prayed and rebuked the storm from our house, and it went over.

When I woke up, I got down on my knees and began to pray for the safety of my wife and children, who were at home during this time.

I will never forget this. I went to the service that morning. Several hundred people were there, and I shared the dream with them. I asked them to agree with me for the safety of my family. I was not aware of anything about the situation, but I had had this dream, and I didn't know what to do about it, so I prayed. As far as I knew the weather was normal at home, so there was nothing to be concerned about. I had talked to my wife on the phone that morning and everything was fine. I went back for the evening service and ministered again.

After the service was over, I returned to my room and laid down to sleep. However, I was not sleepy, so I turned on the television to see the news. I had no more than turned on the set when a "Special Bulletin" flashed over it. It told of a severe tornado that had touched down in the small town in Alabama where I lived.

Immediately I picked up the phone and called my wife. She began to tell me what had taken place. We lived on top of Lookout Mountain, right on the bluff. She said everything got very dark, and a big tornado began moving toward our house. All at once, it turned. A small tornado then broke off that one and started toward our house. The big one sucked the small one back into itself and it came toward our house once more. It would get close, and then go back, as if it was hitting a wall. This happened three times. It finally went about three miles north of our house and moved across the mountain.

Not one thing that was in or around our house was damaged. God does not always give us a word of wisdom when danger is ahead, but most of the time **He will warn us, if we are listening.** Thank God, I heard Him that time.

If you are sensitive to God, I believe He will speak to you and show you things concerning your own future, job, and business. He will give you a word of His wisdom. Don't confuse a word of God's wisdom with the ordinary wisdom to live your life and deal with everyday situation.

If any of you lack wisdom, let him ask of God, that giveth to all men liberally, and upbraideth not; and it shall be given him. (James 1:5)

James is saying here that God will give you this wisdom liberally. God will cause you to become wise; all you have to do is ask Him. Proverbs tells us that wisdom is better than silver or gold.

But of him are ye in Christ Jesus, who of God is made unto us wisdom... (1st Corinthians 1:30)

Meditation in the Word and prayer will cause this wisdom to become active in your life. Paul said in First Corinthians 12:8, *For to one is given by the Spirit the word of wisdom;*

The way he says it here shows you that not all will have the word of wisdom. The Holy Spirit gives it you at His will.

This does not mean for you to throw up your hands and say, "There's no hope for me." I am not implying that at all. Your part is to make yourself available, and as the Holy Spirit wills, He will give you a word of His wisdom.

First Corinthians 12:31 says, *"but covet earnestly the best gifts"*. The best gift is the one that is needed the most at that time.

This gift is associated with the ministry of a prophet. As a matter of fact, it is a great part of his ministry, or makes up a great deal of it. When I speak of the ministry of a prophet, I am not speaking of the gift of prophecy. The gift of prophecy does not look into the future. First Corinthians 14:3 says, *"But he that prophesieth speaketh unto men to edification, and exhortation, and comfort."*

Paul is saying that the gift of prophecy by itself does not speak of the future. It speaks of the things already spoken in God's Word. It exhorts, comforts and edifies you.

Remember that the word of wisdom is a supernatural manifestation in which God gives you a glimpse into the future for special purpose.

Chapter 14

THE WORD OF KNOWLEDGE

The word of knowledge is not the type of knowledge that you receive when hearing the Word taught, reading books, or meditating in the Word of God. It is a supernatural manifestation that brings your attention to something that is very important.

You are enlightened by the Spirit. Revelation comes to you about a situation that you would not have known, other than by this manifestation of the Spirit. It could be a message from God to encourage you; or it could be a revelation to stop something that Satan is plotting against you.

Second Kings 6:8-12 is a unique story. Here the word of knowledge was manifested in Elisha. Syria was at war with Israel. The King of Syria said, "We will set up an ambush."

Revelation of this plot was given to Elisha. Immediately, he warned the King of Israel. The King sent a scout to check this out, and sure enough, the Syrians were waiting.

This happened several times. It kept the Israelites from being slaughtered. The Syrian King thought someone in his camp was informing the Israelites, but one of his officers spoke up and said, "It is none of us. It is the prophet Elisha. He tells the King of Israel the things that you speak in the privacy of your bedroom."

You don't have to be a king to have God send a prophet to you, or to give you a word of knowledge, or to give a word to someone you know. God will minister to you just as He will to anyone else. Acts 10:34 says, *"God is no respecter of persons."*

In First Kings fourteen, King Jeroboam's son Abijah was very sick. At the time, Jeroboam was in a backslidden state. He told his wife to disguise herself so that no one would be able to recognize her. He told her to go to the prophet Ahijah, take him some gifts, and ask him if their son would recover.

The prophet was old and could not see. But while she was on her way to his house, the Lord, by a word of knowledge, told him that the Queen was coming to see him, and that she was pretending to be someone else. He told her why she was coming.

When Ahijah heard her at the door, he said, "Come in, wife of Jeroboam." He told her that her son would die, and also, that the king would have destruction come upon him.

The Word of Knowledge

The word of knowledge and the word of wisdom were both at work in this story. The word of knowledge reveals the past, the present, or both; while the word of wisdom is for the future. You can see how both the present and the future were involved here.

Many times, there are no absolute distinctions between the word of wisdom and the word of knowledge. I can define and tell you what each gift means, show you the scriptures where these gifts are involved, and give you the parameters in which they fall. But I cannot tell you where one ends, and the other begins. You must see how they overlap, as you mature in your knowledge of the gifts.

For to one is given by the Spirit the word of wisdom; to another the word of knowledge by the same Spirit. (1st Corinthians 12:8)

The Spirit will divide the gifts as He desires to. Why can't we have them anytime we want them?

I don't know. I do know this, though. You will only experience them in your life when there is an effort made on your part. First, make yourself available; then exercise your faith in the area of need. You can't make it happen; the Spirit takes care of that.

The three revelation gifts--the word of wisdom, the word of knowledge, and the discerning of spirits--all flow together. There are times when you will not be able to tell which one is at work. The important thing is for you to give opportunity to whichever one it may be.

The word of knowledge can also come through a vision, as shown in Acts 9:10-16. The Lord spoke to Ananias in a vision.

11 And the Lord said unto him, Arise, and go into the street which is called Straight, and enquire in the house of Judas for one called Saul of Tarsus: for behold, he prayeth,

12 And hath seen in a vision a man named Ananias coming in, and putting his hand on him, that he might receive his sight.

15 ...Go thy way: for he is a chosen vessel unto me, to bear my name before the Gentiles, and kings, and the children of Israel:

16 For I will show him how great things he must suffer for my name's sake. (Acts 9:11-12,15-16)

Here again, the present and future are involved, so we know both the word of knowledge and the word of wisdom are at work here.

In Acts 10:19-20 there is yet another example of the word of knowledge. Peter had a vision while on the housetop. While he was thinking about the vision, the Spirit said,

19 ...Behold, three men seek thee.

20 Arise therefore, and get thee down, and go with them, doubting nothing: for I have sent them. (Acts 10:19-20)

Jesus also ministered by the word of knowledge, when He met the Samaritan woman at the well. He asked her for a drink of water. She was surprised that Jesus would even speak to her, and she made a remark about him talking to her. Jesus told her that He would give her,

10 ...living water.

14 ...whosoever drinketh of the water that I shall give him shall never thirst; but the water that I shall give him shall be in him a well of water springing up into everlasting life.

15 The woman saith unto him, Sir, give me this water, that I thirst not, neither come hither to draw.

16 Jesus saith unto her, Go, call thy husband, and come hither.

17 The woman answered and said, I have no husband. Jesus said unto her, Thou hast well said, I have no husband:

18 For thou hast had five husbands; and he whom thou now hast is not thy husband: in that saidst thou truly.

19 The woman saith unto him, Sir, I perceive that thou art a prophet. (John 4:10,14-19)

Revelation can come to you in many ways. It can come by an impression or knowing, as it was with Jesus with the woman at the well, or it can come through tongues and interpretation, or prophecy.

I have witnessed the gift of the word of knowledge many times in my crusades. In Florida once, in an evening meeting, the Lord led me to a lady in the front row. I told her about a physical condition she had. The thing that stood out the most to the woman was that I told her she smoked cigarettes, and I even named the brand. She was very surprised. She pulled out the package, confirming it was the brand I said. I had not guessed, though; I knew.

This built her faith, and she was delivered.

Another time, as I was ministering in Atlanta, I walked up to a man and began to tell him about his past. By revelation knowledge, I told him that he was an alcoholic and had become a prisoner to it. Then I spoke out his name. He began to weep, and he accepted Jesus Christ as his Lord. He was completely delivered!

Very few times in my ministry has the Lord given me a person's name, but quite frequently He has revealed to me the sickness or problems that people have.

Kathryn Kuhlman ministered mostly by the gifts of the Spirit. By impression, she would speak out the name of a disease. The Lord would not necessarily show her who it was, but many would come forward and be healed of the disease she named.

I remember once when I was ministering in Chicago, I had an impression or knowing about a woman who was sitting about five rows from the front. I stepped from the platform and began to speak to her. I told her she had come seeking Jesus, and seeking healing. I also told her that she had been a chain-smoker for years. Tears began to run down her face. She was a Catholic, but that evening she received Jesus as her Savior, a marvelous healing, and deliverance from cigarettes! She had smoked four to five packs a day for 45 years. She also received the Holy Spirit.

The Word is always the most important thing. Don't seek a gift above God's Word. There are people who minister by the wrong spirit. Many follow after them because they were told something about themselves.

I have been used greatly by several of the gifts; but most of all, I teach the Word. I do not want people coming

The Word of Knowledge

to my meetings seeking a sign or a gift. Beware, when you go to a meeting and the person in charge puts all of the attention on the gifts. I believe the body of Christ should have the teaching of the Word as well as the manifestation of the gifts. The gifts of the Spirit are never to take the place of the Word of God. The Bible says you will know a ministry by the fruit it produces.

In First Thessalonians 5:12, Paul says to know them that labor among you. Yes, it is impossible to know very many. Because of the size of their ministries, they are busy with meetings. Then they move on to the next city. They have many responsibilities, and can't stop to meet privately with people. But you can see the fruits of these ministries, and see the kind of people they are with. That will give you some insight.

Now I will say again that I have been used greatly in the gifts. So I have sound advice in these matters. Just because someone tells you your name, address, and many other personal things, don't be persuaded or moved. Don't change the pattern of your life just because of someone else's words. Let such experiences **confirm** what is in your spirit--for God will always tell **you** directly, and only sometimes tells others to confirm this to you. And make sure it is not just an emotional experience.

But instead, **follow the Word**, and you will not miss!

Chapter 15

THE GIFT OF DISCERNING OF SPIRITS

The gift of discerning of spirits seems to be more limited than the other two revelation gifts. This gift certainly does have its place in the body of Christ, though, and it is very important. Discerning of spirits is probably the least talked about and most misunderstood gift.

Some people call it "the gift of discernment," but it's not. It is the gift of the discerning of spirits--and there is a big difference between those two wordings.

Keep in mind this is one of the revelation gifts, being very closely associated with the word of wisdom and the word of knowledge, as it also **reveals** something.

Its main objective is to look into, or reveal spirits. It does not reveal only bad spirits, it reveals good spirits as well.

The Power Of God's Character

There are examples of both good spirits and bad spirits in the Bible. In Exodus 33:18-23, Moses asks to see God's glory. God told him, *I will make My goodness pass before you. You cannot see My face, for no man shall see me and live.* God told him to go to a rock, and when His glory passed by, He would hide him in a cleft. He told him that he would see His form or likeness; he would be seeing into the spirit world, and it was a very special experience. He did not actually see God, but His counterpart, which is Spirit.

Another example is found in Isaiah 6:1-4, when Isaiah said, *I saw the Lord sitting on the throne.* The temple was filled with His glory, there were angels in a great chorus singing, "Holy, Holy, Holy is the Lord of Hosts; the whole earth is filled with His glory."

This had to be a great experience that brought encouragement to Isaiah. Remember, the gifts are for profit, and they are for a specific purpose.

Matthew 17:1-3 says Jesus took Peter, James and John to a high mountain, and His face began to shine like the sun and His clothing became dazzling white. Suddenly, Moses and Elijah appeared and were talking with Him. They were seeing into the Spirit world, for Moses and Elijah had been dead for hundreds of years. Evidently Moses was brought up from Paradise. This must have been a very exciting time for Peter, James and John.

> *5 While he yet spake, behold, a bright cloud overshadowed them: and behold a voice out of the cloud, which said, This is my beloved Son, in whom I am well pleased; hear ye him.*
>
> *6 And when the disciples heard it, they fell on their face, and were sore afraid.*

7 And Jesus came and touched them, and said, Arise, and be not afraid. (Matthew 17:5-7)

When the gifts of the Spirit are given, one should not be afraid. They are given to comfort.

Acts 5:1-10 states an example of the discerning of spirits that could be associated with the word of knowledge. Ananias, with his wife Sapphira, sold some property and brought in only part of the money, although they claimed that it was the full price. Peter saw into the realm of the Spirit, and he spoke to Ananias.

3 But Peter said, Ananias, why hath Satan filled thine heart to lie to the Holy Ghost, and to keep back part of the price of the land?

4 Whiles it remained, was it not thine own? and after it was sold, was it not in thine own power? why hast thou conceived this thing in thine heart? thou hast not lied unto men, but unto God.

5 And Ananias hearing these words fell down, and gave up the ghost....

7 And it was about the space of three hours after, when his wife, not knowing what was done, came in.

8 And Peter answered unto her, Tell me whether ye sold the land for so much? And she said, Yea, for so much.

9 Then Peter said unto her, How is it that ye have agreed together to tempt the Spirit of the Lord? behold, the feet of them which have buried thy husband are at the door, and shall carry thee out.

10 Then fell she down straightway at his feet, and yielded up the ghost.... (Acts 5:3-10)

There was great power manifested in the early church. And I believe in these last days, people are hungry and thirsty for God's power to go to work. As a result, we will see greater things than ever before.

I believe there are people today who have set themselves up to stop the outpouring of God's Spirit. They are attempting this is because they are bound with evil spirits.

But we have God's Word and the gifts of the Spirit, and many of you now are going to make yourselves vessels from which God's power can work. I believe you are tired of talking, and desire to do something about it. Paul had the experience of discerning an evil spirit in Acts 13:1-12, when he and Barnabus were teaching together at Paphos. A very intelligent man sent for them because he wanted to hear the Word of God. Elymas the sorcerer opposed them, and tried to keep the man from hearing the Word. But Paul, with the help of the Holy Spirit by discerning of spirits, saw straight through him,

10 And said, O full of all subtilty and all mischief, thou child of the devil, thou enemy of all righteousness, wilt thou not cease to pervert the right ways of the Lord?

11 And now, behold, the hand of the Lord is upon thee, and thou shalt be blind, not seeing the sun for a season....

*12 Then the deputy, when he saw what was done, **believed**, being astonished at the doc-*

The Gift of Discerning of Spirits

trine of the Lord. (Acts 13:10-12)

We need the revelation gifts at work in the church today. We cannot make them manifest themselves. This is up to the Holy Spirit. But only when we do all that we know to do, and expect these gifts, will they be manifested. In chapter two of this book I said the fruit of the Spirit, the gifts of the Spirit, and the five ministry gifts go hand in hand. I did not say, nor did I intend to say that the fruit of the Spirit is supernatural, or on an equal level with the gifts of the Spirit.

I have taught through all of these chapters that the fruit will give you a foundation and will make you a willing candidate for the gifts. As you keep God's character active in your life, you will be more used of God.

Yes, there are those who have had much of His love, but very little power; while some have had much power, but they never seemed to last. Others have gotten confused, failed early, or have been filled with pride. However, as you keep God's character, you can have His power, if you desire it, and won't fall by the wayside.

In my early years of ministry, I took a church as interim Pastor. While pastoring, I heard of an evangelist who was really having great meetings. He could prophesy like an angel, and his words were extremely persuasive. He drew people in like a magnet.

I went to see him, because everyone spoke of how great he was. When I got there and saw the size of the crowd, I was impressed. But when I saw him, I felt a real coldness. There was so much going on--ministering, prophesying--and people were excited.

So I said to myself, "Oh well, it's just me."

The Power Of God's Character

I was young in the ministry, and was a young man. During the meeting I was introduced to the man. As I was introduced, a very disturbing feeling registered within me. My spirit did not agree with his spirit at all. But I would not listen to my spirit, because other ministers who had been in the ministry much longer than I were approving of his ministry.

Every time went to hear him, I really sensed something was wrong. I kept pushing it aside, though, because he seemed to have everything a person could want. When he ministered, he spoke with such excellence; and you could not help being persuaded by his power.

Against my inward witness, I invited him to speak at my church. He and his wife came. I was torn, but I didn't know what was wrong.

As I was in prayer, all at once, it was as if a light was turned on. I saw a perverted spirit that had bound him. I went to him and told him that the Lord had showed me of his homosexuality. He admitted this, but went on to tell me that he felt it was "Ok". I saw he was deceived and wanted no help from me.

He left the church, of course, but most people would never have believed this about the man.

From the start, my spirit knew. But when the discerning of spirits and the word of knowledge began to work, I was enlightened and set free. This man later divorced his wife, and openly declared that he was a homosexual. He was given nationwide television coverage because of what he had revealed about himself.

The Gift of Discerning of Spirits

The gift of discerning of spirits is given to the body of Christ to give insight into the spirit world and revelation that is beyond our study and meditation of the Word. Thank God for His gifts!

Chapter 16

THE GIFT OF FAITH

To another faith by the same Spirit; to another the gifts of healing by the same Spirit. (1st Corinthians 12:9)

The gift of faith is one of the three power gifts. As I endeavor to explain or define them, in some instances it will be difficult to do, because they are so closely associated. In the Word, I can see places where the gift of faith is at work, accompanied by the working of miracles.

You must first of all understand that the gift of faith, as well as all of the other nine gifts, is supernatural. The best way to describe it would be to say **it's extra faith for a specific time and purpose.** When you come to the end of your faith, then this special faith takes over, as the Spirit wills.

In this study, you must recognize that there are different kinds of faith. There is a natural faith which human beings possess; then there is a saving faith.

For by grace are ye saved through faith; and that not of yourselves: it is the gift of God. (Ephesians 2:8)

Saving faith comes by hearing the Word of God.

So then faith cometh by hearing, and hearing by the word of God. (Romans 10:17)

This means that you hear and understand the Word, then practice it. James 1:22 says, *But be ye doers of the word, and not hearers only...."* When you practice it, you will see God at work in you.

Some people go from meeting to meeting seeking a gift. The gifts are good, and are for you. But don't just wait on the spiritual gifts alone. Take the Word of God daily and apply it to every situation. Then if the Holy Spirit ministers to you by a gift, praise the Lord! Otherwise, continue in the faith walk until you have the answer.

In First Kings seventeen, Elijah told Ahab there would be no rain for three years. This was the gift of faith. I can also see the word of wisdom at work here, because he saw into the future. The gift of miracles was given here to stop the rain.

After this, God told Elijah to hide himself by the brook Cherith that is before Jordan. God told him that he would send the ravens to feed him. The supernatural was at work here again; the gift of faith for Elijah, and the gift of miracles for the raven to bring the food. After that, the Lord told him to go to Zarephath; "I have a widow there to sustain you."

When he arrived there, the widow was getting some wood for the fire. Elijah spoke to her and asked her for a drink of water. As she was going to get water for him, he said, "Fix me some bread."

She replied to the man of God, "I have only enough for my son and me. Actually, it is our last meal."

Elijah said, "Fix mine first."

She did, and because of this, there was then enough for her son and herself.

Here again were two gifts in operation: the gift of faith to tell her to fix the bread, and the gift of miracles to multiply the meal each day until the rain came.

In the meantime, her son died. The woman called Elijah in, and he prayed for the boy, who was raised from the dead by the supernatural gifts of God. In this chapter, several gifts operated through Elijah, and you can see how they overlap and work together.

I believe the subject of raising the dead needs some attention given to it. I believe raising the dead is scriptural. I will say this, that I don't totally understand it; and I don't really know if anyone alive today fully understands it either. At this point in my ministry, I have never had a dead person be raised. I do believe it takes the supernatural gifts for a person to be raised from the dead. Kenneth E. Hagin says it takes all three of the power gifts to raise someone from the dead: **the gift of faith** to bring their spirit back in their body; **the gift of miracles** to raise or stand them up; and **the gift of healing** to heal them of the disease or condition that caused them to die. I believe this to be true.

There has been some confusion about the dead being raised. However, I showed you where Elijah raised the dead. There are other Old Testament examples of where the dead were raised. It is not impossible with God. In Matthew 10:8, Jesus told the apostles to raise the dead. In Mark five, Jesus raised Jairus' daughter from the dead. Luke seven tells this story about Jesus.

> *12 Now when he came nigh to the gate of the city, behold, there was a dead man carried out, the only son of his mother, and she was a widow: and much people of the city was with her.*
>
> *13 And when the Lord saw her, he had compassion on her, and said unto her, Weep not. 14 And he came and touched the bier: and they that bare him stood still. And he said, Young man, I say unto thee, Arise.*
>
> *15 And he that was dead sat up, and began to speak. And he delivered him to his mother.* (Luke 7:12-15)

In John eleven, Jesus raised Lazarus after he had been dead four days! In Acts 20:9-12, Paul was preaching and a young man fell out of the window. The fall took his life. Paul raised him from the dead. The prophets raised the dead. Jesus told his Apostles to. Jesus did, and the Apostles did.

I have read of other men of God who have raised the dead. One was Smith Wigglesworth. I was never privileged to see or hear him, only to read about him. According to reports, he was a man of great faith. Many outstanding healings and supernatural miracles took place during his ministry. The reports of his life said that he raised three people from the dead in his ministry. Apparently he did not raise every dead person that he came

The Gift of Faith

in contact with, but according to the reports, he did it three times.

I don't believe it is always God's will for a person to be raised from the dead. I am not suggesting that you are not to pray for the dead to be raised. However, if you don't believe, there certainly is no use in praying. I have heard of cases where people have refused to bury a person's body for several days, because they were praying for them to be raised. There are other instances where people had no emotional involvement and very little compassion in a situation. They would advise someone to pray for the loved one to be raised from the dead. When nothing happened, it caused hurt feelings, frustration, disappointment, and discouragement. The person then felt as if they had done something wrong. They lived with condemnation, and felt like a failure.

This should not be. If you pray and do all you know to do, and life is not restored, you should leave it in the hands of God.

Sometimes, people have the desire to go on and be with the Lord. Their friends and family who are "Word people" have them confessing, *By His stripes I am healed*.

They can confess this a thousand times a day, but if their desire is to go and be with the Father, their confessing the Word isn't doing anything but satisfying the ears of the people who have told the sick person to quote scripture. So trying to bring back a person whose will is to go and be with the Lord would be useless. When a person is born again and at peace with God, it is always a victory for that person when they graduate from this life to the one we are all working and waiting for in heaven. They do not want to return here.

When a person dies suddenly because of an accident or a disease, and they had not lived a full life here, it is natural not to want to let them go. But in some cases, there should not even be an attempt to raise them; just let them go.

Each individual situation should have prompting from the Holy Spirit.

I was speaking in Houston in a campmeeting. At the end of the service, a lady was brought up to me for prayer. She was having a heart attack. All at once, it was as if I was another person. I spoke forcefully for her to be healed. I commanded her heart to be healed. She had been in so much pain, she could hardly breathe. But all at once she stood up, the expression on her face changed, and she began walking around and praising the Lord, and shouting, "I am healed!"

Two gifts were in operation: the gift of faith and the gift of healing. Her heart was healed.

In 1968 I rented a large building for a revival crusade in Chattanooga, Tennessee. A few days after the meeting began, I felt a strong leading to fast. This was a very special meeting, and each night there was demonstration of God's power. The meeting had continued for 18 days.

That evening, I noticed a woman walking down the aisle. She barked like a dog, hissed like a snake, and made all kinds of noises. She was possessed by the devil. I knew her because, in my youth, she had attended the same church I did. She would act strangely in services and cause so much disturbance that the pastor would call the

The Gift of Faith

police. It took more than ten strong men to put her in the police car and take her to the psychiatric ward. Sometimes she became so violent that she would hurt a guest speaker.

Knowing all of this while I was standing on the platform, and having had nothing to eat for 18 days--to tell you the truth, I was afraid of her. I didn't know what to do, so I began to praise the Lord as I walked across the platform. I said, "Hosanna to the King. Hosanna to the King." (This means, O save; it is also an exclamation of adoration.) However, I did not know the meaning at the time I was saying it. I just praised, and shouted it for a few minutes; the people then stood on their feet and praised, and shouted it with me.

All at once, I felt like a different person. I jumped off the stage and went directly to this woman. I put my hand on her head, and she said, "Boooooy, get --- your --- hands ---off --- me!"

Somehow, what she said, and the way she said it did not bother me. It didn't even register within me. I was no longer afraid. I looked around and saw an empty chair on the second row. I said to her, "I command you in Jesus' Name to go to that seat, sit down, and never again disturb my service, or bother me."

Like a little lamb, she went to that seat and sat down. She never moved or opened her mouth in that service. She also came to other people's services, but never bothered them. This was very unusual; it had never happened before. If you even touched her, she had so much energy that she would hit you and hurt you, or pick you up and throw you.

The Power Of God's Character

This time, the gift of faith was given to me, and it controlled her. And you can cast out demon spirits by the gift of faith.

I was awakened one night from my sleep by the Holy Spirit. He told me to pray for a man that I knew. I knew some of his situation. He and his wife had walked with God. Many circumstances had come their way, and they had ceased going to church. They had given up their prayer life and had lost fellowship with God. From there, their marriage began to deteriorate, and they ended up getting a divorce. They were both living in separate states, and living different lives.

I knew this and thought there was little hope of their getting back together because of the lifestyle they had chosen.

When God told me to pray for him, I didn't really know how, so I prayed in tongues for at least an hour. When I stopped, I sensed victory. I went back to bed, closed my eyes, and fell asleep immediately, as if a light switch had been turned off. This was unusual for me. I got up the next day and never gave much thought to it.

Several days passed. I was driving over 100 miles to speak in a service and was praying in tongues as I went. The Spirit of God was strong upon me.

All at once, the Spirit of God said to go where this man worked, and pray for him.

I looked at my watch and said, "Lord, his business will be closed."

But God knew so much more than I did. He said, "If I tell you to go pray for him, he will be there."

The Gift of Faith

I followed God's instruction. I made an exit off the interstate and drove up to his place of business. He was there and was just closing up. I had a few words with him, just small talk.

All at once, the Spirit of God rose up on the inside of me, and I felt like I was nine feet tall! I spoke forcefully to him.

"Get your life straight with God right now!"

He began to cry, and made peace with God right there in his place of business.

A few minutes later, I thought of what had come over me; it was the gift of faith.

After this happened, I spent time talking with him, and told him to go back to his wife.

He told me that he no longer loved her, and that she did not love him, so it was useless to even think about it.

I continued to pray for him, and within several weeks, he and his wife were back together. She renewed her relationship with God. And one year later, they had another child. The last I heard of them, they were happier than they had ever been before!

Some years ago, I was in Canada in a crusade. That night I was praying for people who had eye problems. A man wearing glasses stood in front of me. Suddenly, I grabbed his glasses, threw them on the floor, and broke them.

He was healed! Working together was the gift of faith an the gift of healing.

Another man who was standing nearby saw what happened. He took off his glasses, threw them against the wall and broke them; but nothing happened. He just did it of himself.

You can't make it happen. It is as the Spirit wills.

I have had many experiences with the gift of faith. I encourage you to tune yourself in to God, and be used by the gift of faith.

In Samuel, look at how David was used by the gift of faith. He slew a lion and a bear. When Goliath was defying the army of God, David said, "This uncircumcised Philistine shall be as the bear and the lion." He picked up five stones, and by the power of God (the gift of faith), he ran towards the giant, released a stone, and delivered Israel from the hand of the Philistines.

Great things can and will take place as the body of Christ prepares for this. In defining these power gifts, remember that they are all closely associated. You could see why there could be more than one at work in the examples we have looked at in the Word.

I look at Robert Tilton in Dallas. What a great work he is doing. I marvel every time I go and see some of the things that he does for God. One day, while sitting with him in his office, we were talking about his ministry. All at once, I realized that the majority of what he has done has been beyond his faith. It is supernatural faith, the gift of faith working in his ministry.

Don't limit God! He will give you the gift of faith in your business, your job, and your home, to bring glory and honor to the kingdom of God. Exercise your faith now for this marvelous gift to be at work in you. It will bring great change in your life. I believe the gift of faith will bring deliverance to nations. It will take control and move all obstacles out of the way.

Faith is the opposite of fear. When you make room for this gift, it will open doors that you could never open. I believe in these last days, as people give themselves to God, many will be used of God by the gift of faith. They will be empowered to go into places with the gospel that they could never have gone to on their own ability.

For the weapons of our warfare are not carnal, but mighty through God to the pulling down of strongholds. (2nd Corinthians 10:4)

The gifts of the Spirit are weapons. They are beyond your faith or ability. The gifts of the Spirit--along with prayer--will pull down strongholds. I believe, as the body of Christ begins to willingly intercede, it will bring the supernatural demonstration of God's power on the scene as never before. It will not be just one man, it will be many. If it were just one man, people would get their eyes on him. But it is for all.

Remember, compassion and intercession are the keys. They remove selfishness. Intercede for the demonstration of God's power.

Chapter 17

THE GIFT OF WORKING OF MIRACLES

The gift of working of miracles alters nature. It has the power to multiply food and divide a sea of water. It moves upon the natural in a supernatural way, and changes things that would not happen by natural means.

Today, people call many things miracles. In one sense, they may be. However, we are examining the gift of working of miracles that is given by the Holy Spirit for a specific time and purpose. Some people confuse the gift of healing with the gift of working of miracles. When someone is healed instantly, this is not the working of miracles, it is the gift of healing.

Sometimes when I think about the telephone and television, they seem to me like miracles. Also I think of a satellite; a picture is sent out from them to earth and is transmitted to a satellite thousands of miles into outer space. Then a receiving station on earth brings the signal back to earth, and you see that same picture on a television set.

But this is not the gift of working of miracles, because this is the ability of man at work with tools.

The gift of working of miracles is God's ability at work here in the natural realm. No man can duplicate it or make it work; it is by the Holy Spirit.

In the Old Testament, Moses was used many times by the gift of working of miracles. God told him to throw down his rod; it became a serpent. He picked it up by the tail, and it became a rod again. He dealt with Pharaoh with the gift of working of miracles. When Moses and the children of Israel came to the Red Sea, it divided and they went across on dry land. This was the gift of working of miracles.

> *So the people shouted when the priests blew with the trumpets: and it came to pass, when the people heard the sound of the trumpet, and the people shouted with a great shout, that the wall fell down flat, so that the people went up into the city, every man straight before him, and they took the city.* (Joshua 6:20)

The Bible says the walls fell flat. They didn't just fall down. If they had, the people would not have been able to go in because of all the debris. They fell flat, which allowed the Israelites to go into the city easily and take it.

In Second Kings 6:5-7, Elisha made an ax head come to the surface after it had fallen into the water.

The Gift of Working of Miracles

Many times, Jesus demonstrated the gift of working of miracles. The first time in his ministry was in John, chapter two, when He turned the water into wine. This was a miracle. If you take grape juice and let it ferment, that is not a miracle.

Mark 4:39 says "a great storm of wind" tossed the ship to and fro. Jesus said, *Peace, be still.* The wind obeyed, and the storm calmed. That was a miracle.

In Matthew 17:27, Jesus and Peter needed money to pay taxes at the temple. Jesus told Peter to go fishing, and if he would look in the mouth of the first fish he caught, he would find money. "Pay the taxes with it," he told Peter. This, indeed, was a miracle.

In Matthew 14:22-33, Jesus told His disciples to get in their boat and cross to the other side of the lake, while He stayed to get the people home, and to pray a while. But in the night the disciples were troubled because of the storm. Jesus came to them, walking on the water. Peter asked Jesus if he could come to Him. He had started toward Jesus, when he got his eyes on the wind and waves of the sea, and began to sink. But Jesus picked him up out of the water. It takes the gift of working of miracles to walk on the water.

In Luke 5:4-7, Jesus used Peter's boat to do some preaching. Peter had fished all night and didn't catch anything. Jesus told him to go into deeper water and let down his nets. When he did this, he caught so many fish that it almost caused his boat to sink. This was the working of miracles.

In Acts 5:19-20, the Apostles had been healing the sick and performing signs and wonders.

The Power Of God's Character

The Sadducees and the High Priest became jealous of them and had them arrested and put into jail. But the angel of the Lord came and opened the door for them, and they went to the temple and began to preach again.

In Acts 12:7-11, Peter was in jail. The following day he was to be executed. He was double-chained between two soldiers while others were standing guard. An angel came into the prison, awoke Peter from his sleep, and told him to get up. As he did, the chains fell off his wrists. Peter went outside and made his way to an all-night prayer meeting.

It was indeed a miracle for the chains to fall off Peter's wrist, and for the sixteen soldiers not to know anything about it.

The days of miracles are not past.

Chapter 18

THE GIFTS OF HEALING

First Corinthians 12:9 says, *"to another the gifts of healing by the same Spirit."*

The gifts of healing is one of the power gifts. In many cases, it is closely associated with the gift of faith. The gifts of healing brings instant healing to people, without the aid of any type of medical help.

I am not against medicine. I believe in doctors, and I encourage people to have themselves checked after they have been prayed for and have received healing.

I have had a very successful healing ministry. I have seen many people healed by God's supernatural power. However, many people fail to understand the difference between a gift of healing and a gradual healing.

Both can come by having hands laid on you. But many people, when they don't receive instant healing, get discouraged and do not think they were healed.

Every type of healing was purchased at Calvary. First Peter 2:24 says, *"by whose (Jesus') stripes ye were healed."* Jesus took every sickness upon Himself, that we might not have to suffer. Mark 16:18 says, *"they shall lay hands on the sick, and they shall recover."* James 5;14-15 says this.

14 Is any sick among you? let him call for the elders of the church; and let them pray over him, anointing him with oil in the name of the Lord:

15 And the prayer of faith shall save the sick, and the Lord shall raise him up; and if he have committed sins, they shall be forgiven him. (James 5:14-15)

None of these scriptures tell you to pray, "...if it be thy will." They tell you to lay hands on the sick, and **they will** recover. It is God's will to heal everyone. I don't know why not everyone gets healed by the gifts of healing, but I do know that God heals.

When I am praying for people in a service and have a special anointing upon me, I usually stop and ask the person I prayed for if there is any noticeable change in their condition. I am not doubting my prayer, I am checking to see if they were healed by the gifts of healing.

If they are healed by the gifts of healing, it will be instant. If they are not healed by the gifts of healing, then they will recover over a period of time.

In a crusade at Chattanooga some years ago, a lady had been helped into the meeting. She had had a stroke, and the doctors told her there was nothing more they could do for her.

The Gifts of Healing

I walked back into the crowd and told her to get up. I did not know how serious her condition was, but I spoke again with such authority that it was as if I was a different person. Actually, the gift of faith had come upon me. When I spoke the second time, she began to get up, and she hobbled a couple of steps.

All at once her body was loosed. She could walk perfectly. And then she began to run and praise the Lord! She was so excited about her healing, for over 15 minutes she controlled the service.

In Matthew eight, a leper came to Jesus and worshipped Him, saying, *If thou wilt, thou canst make me clean.* Jesus put forth His hand and touched him, saying, *"I will; be thou clean."* Immediately the leper was cleansed.

This was a gift of healing. I have known many men who have been used of God with the gifts of healing. Some have seemed to have great results for deaf ears; others for blind eyes. I know in my ministry, I seem to have more people healed of deafness than any other condition.

Once I was in Cape Town, South Africa, in a crusade. While I was speaking, a lady stood to her feet and began to shout, disturbing the service. I walked off the platform and finaly got her calmed down. She told me she had been in an automobile accident five years ago, and had become deaf as a result. As she was sitting there, the power of God went through her and opened her ears, and she began to hear perfectly.

Many other people then came running to the front of the auditorium, testifying of healing that had taken place in them. A great outpouring of God's Spirit came upon the people there, and the gift of God healed hundreds of people that night.

I can remember as a young evangelist, I would travel to any crusade where I could see and hear A.A. Allen. He had one of the greatest healing ministries. I desired to just be close to him, and have him lay hands on me every time I could get him to. I wanted the gifts of healing so that I could bring help to the hurting. Gifts can be received by the laying on of hands, and I believe he actually did transmit his anointing upon me, and many others.

Second Timothy says this.

Wherefore I put thee in remembrance that thou stir up the gift of God, which is in thee by the putting on of my hands. (2nd Timothy 1:6)

Paul laid his hands on Timothy and stirred up the gifts that were in him. This is the reason why I have always desired those who have special gifts to lay their hands on me, to stir up the gifts within me. Then I lay my hands on others, expecting them to receive their healing.

I have always known that it is not me doing the work. I know it is God's supernatural power, and I always give God the glory and credit. The more people I see healed by God's power, the more I humble myself and thank Him for using me in helping someone else.

One night in a large crusade in Brazil, I was speaking under a powerful anointing. I began to call out different sicknesses by the word of knowledge, and many people were being healed.

A lady who was over 90 years old was brought to the front, and I was told she was blind. All at once, she began to shout in her language, "I can see! I can see!" There

The Gifts of Healing

were close to 15,000 people there that night, and many received instant healings.

I believe the Word of God. You believe it right now, and ask God to use you with the gifts of healing to help someone.

Don't play games. God's power is real. In John 14, Jesus tells you to do the works that He did. In First Corinthians 12:31, Paul said to covet the best gifts. Ask God for His power. You can change the world by demonstrating His great power.

> *29 And Jesus departed from thence, and came night unto the sea of Galilee; and went up into a mountain, and sat down there.*
>
> *30 And great multitudes came unto him, having with them those that were lame, blind, dumb, maimed, and many others, and cast them down at Jesus' feet; and he healed them:*
>
> *31 Insomuch that the multitude wondered, when they saw the dumb to speak, the maimed to be whole, the lame to walk, and the blind to see: and they glorified the God of Israel.* (Matthew 15:29-31)

Jesus demonstrated the gifts of healing here. The power of God is still the same as it was when Jesus healed those people in the scripture above. The problem is that many people have limited God. They only talk of the past and look to the future of heaven. God wants us to use His power **now** to set the captives free, to open the eyes of the blind, and to cast out demon spirits. I believe God wants everyone to lay hands on the sick and do the works of Jesus Christ.

One day, while walking, Peter and John came to a man who was lying at the gate of the temple and begging for money.

Peter said to him, *Silver and gold have I none; but such as I have give I thee: in the name of Jesus Christ of Nazareth rise up and walk.*

Peter took him by the hand and lifted him up, and immediately his feet and ankle bones received strength. The man was healed by the gifts of healing.

Intercession is one of the keys that will produce that supernatural power. You can't just sit down and hope for it; you must be busy about the things of God. You must believe that He is a "right now" God. I believe the church is in store for the greatest things it has ever seen in the supernatural gifts of God.

15 Insomuch that they brought forth the sick into the streets, and laid them on beds and couches, that at least the shadow of Peter passing by might overshadow some of them.

16 There came also a multitude out of the cities round about unto Jerusalem, bringing sick folks, and them which were vexed with unclean spirits: and they were healed every one. (Acts 5:15-16)

The Bible says, in the last days God will pour out of His Spirit upon all flesh. I believe now is the time to expect God to use you. Through Jesus, you have been made righteous. *For he hath made him to be sin for us, who knew no sin; that we might be made the righteousness of God in him.* (2nd Corinthians 5:21) The work has been done at Calvary. Through the work of the cross, you

The Gifts of Healing

have been made worthy.

Don't let Satan make you believe you are not good enough. If you pray for someone and see no change, go to the next person and pray the prayer of faith. The only way God will use you is if you desire to be used of Him. In First Corinthians 12:31, you are admonished to covet (or desire) spiritual gifts. God will not give you something you do not want.

There is a need **now** in the body of Christ for the gifts of the Spirit; and it does not have to be only in the church that these supernatural gifts are demonstrated. It could be in a place of business. Give yourself to Him, and desire spiritual gifts.

In defining the gifts, I can show you what they do and how they may be obtained. The rest is up to you. Make the effort to be used. And remember, you do not have to hold an office of one of the five ministry gifts in order to have the gifts of healing operate in your life.

If you are a lay person, you should be submitted to your Pastor. In a church service, the gifts should be demonstrated through the leadership of those who are in charge of the service.

You may ask, "Where could my gifts be used?" They can be used out where the people are. The Bible says to go out into the highways and hedges.

When I was a teenager and had no place to minister, I went to the hospital and witnessed and prayed for all who desired my prayers. Remember, you must have the desire. Find those who are in need and want help, and give it to them.

34 Then shall the King say unto them on his right hand, Come, ye blessed of my Father, inherit the kingdom prepared for you from the foundation of the world:

35 For I was an hungred, and ye gave me meat: I was thirsty, and ye gave me drink: I was a stranger, and ye took me in:

36 Naked, and ye clothed me: I was sick, and ye visited me: I as in prison, and ye came unto me.

37 Then shall the righteous answer him, saying, Lord, when saw we thee an hungred, and fed thee? or thirsty, and gave thee drink?

38 When saw we thee a stranger, and took thee in? or naked, and clothed thee?

39 Or when saw we thee sick, or in prison, and came unto thee?

40 And the King shall answer and say unto them, Verily I say unto you, Inasmuch as ye have done it unto one of the least of these my brethren, ye have done it unto me. (Matthew 25:34-40)

Jesus is saying to you, go help anyone who is in need. If you go to them and they receive you, minister to them. If not, don't take it personally; go to the next person who desires help. The world is crying out for help.

John was a voice crying out in the wilderness saying, "Prepare ye the way of the Lord." He said, "I am not Jesus, but He is coming."

John saw Him and said,

The Gifts of Healing

Behold the Lamb of God, which taketh away the sin of the world. (John 1:29)

The Holy Spirit descended upon Jesus as John baptized Him. Soon Jesus performed His first miracle. He took 162 gallons of water and turned it into wine. When Jesus matured and came into his ministry, He went forth doing the works of God.

Find out what your calling is and get into it. Don't say, "Well, I'll leave it up to someone else." No, do your part.

You may be an intercessor, or God may choose to use you in another way. But whatever you do, make yourself available to be used of God by His supernatural gifts.

There are practicing doctors and dentists now who are filled with the Holy Spirit. They lay their hands on the sick and see them healed by the power of God. Many of these doctors are being used by the gifts of healings.

A member of my church who is a dentist shared this story with me. His youngest daughter (age 9) is baptized in the Holy Spirit. She knows about God's power to heal miraculously, and has experienced its operation in her life. In the latter part of 1982, she was in to see her father for a regular cleaning and check up. After X-rays were taken, two cavities were found.

Normal procedure would have been to just set up an appointment to have the two teeth restored.

This time, however, routine wasn't followed. She asked her father to lay hands on her and pray for those teeth to be healed. He did so, and she left his office believing she was totally whole.

The time between the cleaning appointment and the one for restoration was four days. When she entered the office for the fillings, she made an unusual request. She asked that another x-ray be taken of where the cavities were. Her father did, and when his assistant, who had taken the first one, developed that film, she began to shout and praise the Lord. There were no cavities visible anywhere. Two perfectly healthy teeth were on the X-ray.

I believe the gifts of healing was in operation when her father laid his hands upon her. The entire family rejoices continually for the miracles of God.

I have witnessed the gifts of God at work in many different ways. One example: I have prayed over a prayer cloth, held it close to my body, and the cloth was sent out. Many have testified of supernatural healings taking place after receiving the cloth.

11 And God wrought special miracles by the hands of Paul:

12 So that from his body were brought unto the sick handkerchiefs or aprons, and the diseases departed from them, and the evil spirits went out of them. (Acts 19:11-12)

Once while ministering in a crusade in Canada, a young woman came for prayer. She told me her mother had been in a serious car wreck, and the doctors gave her mother no hope that she would live. She asked me to pray for her.

That evening the gifts of healing had been at work, and I sensed a special anointing upon me. I felt impressed to take my handkerchief out of my pocket, pray over it, and send it with this woman to give to her mother. She

The Gifts of Healing

did, and a situation that looked hopeless changed. She was healed, raised from her death bed, and made whole!

In 1980, I was speaking in a campmeeting in Dallas. I felt especially led to pray and anoint cloths. Paul Landry, who is now a very good friend of mine, was in the service that day. I prayed over a cloth that he had given to me. I want to share with you his words of how it all happened. This is Paul Landry's story:

"My wife, Vergena, had been experiencing some unusual discomfort and pain in her lower abdomen, to the point where she started feeling a hard lump developing. In just a matter of days, it began growing to considerable size, (about the size of a large grapefruit).

The doctor took one quick examination and immediately wanted to set up an appointment for surgery. Both Vergena and I felt checked about it and asked for ten days. We did so because we wanted to give the Great Physician an opportunity to do His work first.

Immediately we came against it in the name of Jesus, and selected a series of verses of scripture to stand upon, believe, and confess.

The next day I left for a campmeeting in Dallas, where I heard Brother Don Clowers share dynamic teaching and preaching on the working of special miracles.

At the conclusion of his message, he felt directed of the Holy Spirit to exercise his faith in accordance with Acts 19, where it says,

11 And God wrought special miracles by the hands of Paul:

12 So that from his body were brought unto the sick handkerchiefs or aprons, and the diseases departed from them, and the evil spirits went out of them. (Acts 19:11-12)

Brother Clowers encouraged people to lay handkerchiefs or pieces of cloth at the altar and allow him to, in the name of Jesus, pray a special healing anointing upon the cloths. Then they were to be carried back to our sick loved ones.

I had heard the mentioning of Acts 19:11-12 before, but never had I seen it shared with such intensity and power. Instantly I thought of my wife, and I reached in my back pocket, pulled out my handkerchief, and laid it on the altar.

Brother Clowers began to pray, and we agreed with him as he began touching and picking up some of the cloths and actually applying some of them to his own head, arms, chest, legs, and various parts of his body. I could not help but notice when he picked up my handkerchief and held it against his lower abdomen. He continued to pray in the spirit and with understanding. He anointed these cloths with supernatural healing virtue. Naturally my faith skyrocketed; something in my heart bore witness to the fact that my wife was now in store for a special miracle, according to His Word.

I will never forget calling Vergena that night and telling her that I had a special surprise for her. I was going to carry her miracle home with me. It sounded a bit funny at first, but I really believed it with all my heart.

Upon arriving at home, we applied that cloth to Vergena's abdomen and agreed together in the name of Jesus for a flow of healing virtue to be transmitted into her body, and bring healing to manifestation, and disappearance of that growth. Nothing happened!

As far as our eyes were concerned, the physical condition actually got a bit worse, rather than better, but we refused to let go of our confession, and now our expression of faith.

My wife actually wore that cloth in such a way that it would be in constant contact with her for two or three days.

It seemed that each day her spiritual strength and physical strength increased.

Finally, on Sunday morning, Vergena woke up to discover that the growth had completely disappeared. It was the day before the expiration of our ten-day grace period granted by our earthly doctor. And praise be to God for honoring His Word and performing a supernatural work on our behalf."

All things are possible to him that believeth. (Mark 9:23)

Let me encourage you to make yourself available for the power gifts to operate in your life.

Chapter 19

THE GIFT OF PROPHECY

> *To another the working of miracles; to another prophecy; to another discerning of spirits; to another divers kinds of tongues; to another the interpretation of tongues.* (1st Corinthians 12:10)

The gift of prophecy is one of the three inspiration gifts. The other two are diverse kinds of tongues and the interpretation of tongues. Of these three, the gift of prophecy is said by the Bible to be the greatest. It is a supernatural utterance inspired by God in a known tongue that edifies, exhorts, and comforts.

> *But he that prophesieth speaketh unto men to edification, and exhortation, and comfort.*
> (1st Corinthians 14:3)

This verse of scripture is very plain in what it says. Paul says the gift of prophecy will edify, build up, exhort, encourage, comfort, or console a person. It will not get into the future, nor does it get into revelation.

The word "prophecy" is used in a very general way. However, in this particular place, I don't want you to misunderstand its meaning or be confused about what the gift of prophecy is.

Some people don't really understand the difference between the ministry of a prophet and the gift of prophecy by itself. The gift of prophecy is one of the gifts which accompany the ministry of a prophet--along with the word of wisdom, the word of knowledge, and the discerning of spirits.

When the gift of prophecy stands alone, it should not be confused with the prophet's ministry. People sometimes see the ministry gift of a prophet; as he prophesies, other gifts become involved. If they try to do what he is doing, they cause confusion.

Prophecy is a beautiful gift and should not be taken lightly. When one is truly used by the Holy Spirit with this gift, it is not given to him to get special attention by a local group of people. Neither should people be drawn to this person to seek a prophecy.

I have known of this happening many times when people have been used with the gift of prophecy. People would call them daily to get a word of comfort; or they would be wanting direction.

Your comfort and direction should come from the Word of God, and from the Holy Spirit.

But the Comforter, which is the Holy Ghost, whom the Father will send in my name, he shall teach you all things, and bring all things to

The Gift of Prophecy

your remembrance. (John 14:26)

You do not have to go to someone else to find out God's will for your life. God will tell you what His will is for you. The gift of prophecy is given for a specific time and purpose. As is true of all the gifts, you cannot turn it on and off any time you want to.

I believe when a gift is manifested in the church, it should be coming primarily through the one in charge of the service. If it doesn't, I believe the one in charge of the service should know by the Spirit that someone has a prophecy, or whatever the gift is that is going to be demonstrated.

The people in a congregation are never to get up and interrupt or disturb that service. God does not work that way. He never confuses.

Let all things be done decently and in order.
(1st Corinthians 14:40)

If there is a gift to be manifested, the one in charge of the meeting can pause and give place to it, and it will bring blessing and encouragement.

I was in Pittsburgh several years ago in a crusade. I began my message, and the Spirit of the Lord was moving upon the people. As I began to minister the Word, a man stood up and began to prophesy. When he did, it shocked me, for what he was saying had nothing to do with my subject. It was my first night, and there was hardly anyone there who knew me. I avoided any confrontation with him. After he sat down, I went on teaching, although it was rather difficult to do; but I managed.

As I stopped to read a scripture, he stood up and spoke out again. It also did not have anything to do with

The Power Of God's Character

what I was teaching about. He spoke for a couple of minutes; then he sat down. I got things under control and began to teach again.

He interrupted me with another prophecy. This time, however, I spoke up and told him that he was out of order. The things he was saying were good, but they were not in line with what I was talking about, so it must have been from him. I told him, furthermore, he was causing confusion, and I asked if he would please be seated.

Now, I would not let that happen again; I would deal with it the first time.

I teach that in a local assembly, if there is a prophecy to be given, the person with the prophecy must get the attention of the one in charge by raising his hand. If he is acknowledged, then he may proceed; if not, he is not to speak.

If it is an inspired message from God, it will remain until its proper time; it doesn't have to be given immediately.

There are those who go to meetings and don't want to respect authority. They say that they can never find a church for their gift to operate in. They want to take a great part of the service by doing their own thing, which is not scriptural. They say they believe in a body ministry.

I do too, but everybody has a head, and all things are done from the head of the body. So it is with the church.

God will not have a man prepare himself, anoint him, and then have him sit through the service and watch the members of the congregation take over. God may use some other seasoned minister, and I believe we should always be open to that. But no one in the congregation

The Gift of Prophecy

should get up and prophesy to different individuals.

I have been in meetings with other ministers when the one who was scheduled to speak for that service did not get to speak, because God used other experienced men of God in the gifts. Everything flowed beautifully, because it was in order.

In these meetings, all should be open for the Holy Spirit to move as He wills. Let me say again, God will not take a stranger in the congregation to stand up and interrupt the service with a gift.

If someone stands up in a public gathering to bring a prophecy, the entire congregation cannot hear; so the prophecy is not able to exhort and comfort all the people. The ones who could not hear it would only be confused. God doesn't act that way.

I am not opposed to prayer groups and Bible studies, as long as they are under the authority of a responsible local pastor who has a way of maintaining order. Beware of the one that does not have the proper oversight, but has a lot of prophecy, and supposedly, other gifts are being manifested. You could get hurt, if you relied on this as being from God.

One thing I really want to point out here is that **God has order**. The gifts are for profit. The Bible says every good and perfect gift is from God. If it is from God, it will edify, comfort, or exhort you. First Thessalonians 5:20 says, *Despise not prophesyings.* Don't quench the Spirit, but prove all things by the Word. Judge prophecy by the Word. Those who are doing the prophesying, even if it's you, should have the character of God in them. If not, it should not be received at all.

People have told me that prophecy is preaching. This is not true. I have preached a lot under a heavy anointing, but it was not prophecy. On the other hand, I have been teaching and preaching, when the gift of prophecy came upon me, and I would prophesy; sometimes for a short period of time, and sometimes for a good while. The length doesn't matter, as long as it is the gift of prophecy. Prophecy will exhort, edify, and comfort.

Sometimes, while in prayer, the gift of prophecy comes upon me, and I prophesy to myself by the Holy Spirit. Sometimes I pray by prophecy.

We need to have the gift of prophecy working, and more than just inside the church. Wherever you are, you can be sensitive to God.

One morning about 6:00 a.m., Leslie Hale and I were riding down the road in Chattanooga. We were on our way to be on a local television talk show. All of a sudden, he began to speak to me under the unction of the Holy Spirit. He told me of some recent events that had been trying to place me under pressure, and what the Lord was going to do about them. Everything he said brought comfort and edification to me, even at six in the morning. This was the word of wisdom and the gift of prophecy being produced together.

Follow after charity, and desire spiritual gifts, but rather that ye may prophesy. (1st Corinthians 14:1)

Paul says to desire spiritual gifts, and he emphasized prophecy. You do not have to be an Apostle, Prophet Evangelist, Pastor or Teacher to prophesy. The gift is available to any Spirit-filled believer.

Sometimes people think there has to be prophecy in every Church service. It is good if God chooses to give one, but if there is not a prophecy in every service, maybe God didn't see a specific need for this gift to operate.

Remember, when any gift is demonstrated, it will always profit.

Chapter 20

DIVERS KINDS OF TONGUES AND INTERPRETATION OF TONGUES

To another the working of miracles; to another prophecy; to another discerning of spirits; to another divers kinds of tongues; to another the interpretation of tongues. (1st Corinthians 12:10)

Divers kinds of tongues and interpretation of tongues are gifts of inspiration. These two gifts actually work side-by-side, and together they equal the gift of prophecy. These two gifts were the only two gifts that were not in operation in the Old Testament, and by Jesus.

Tongues were not given until the day of Pentecost.

2 And suddenly there came a sound from heaven as of a rushing mighty wind, and it filled all the house where they were sitting.

3 And there appeared unto them cloven tongues like as of fire, and it sat upon each of them.

4 And they were all filled with the Holy Ghost, and began to speak with other tongues, as the Spirit gave them utterance. (Acts 2:2-4)

This is the first time people spoke in other tongues. Jesus had already told them in Mark 16:15 that they would. He said, *"they shall speak with new tongues."* It seems there had been some misunderstanding about speaking in tongues. As I said in Chapter 11, you do speak with tongues when you receive the infilling of the Holy Spirit. Your prayer language is important.

The Apostle Paul said in First Corinthians 14:39, *"Forbid not to speak in tongues."* A question often asked is: Is there any difference between your prayer language and giving divers tongues in a public meeting?

Yes. Everyone who is filled with the Holy Spirit is given a language to talk to God with. You do not understand what you are saying, but it is direct communication with God. It is a prayer that bypasses the intellect. Paul said in First Corinthians 14:14 (paraphrased);

When I pray in an unknown tongue, my mind is unfruitful; but my human spirit, by the Holy Spirit that is within me, prays, and this prayer cannot be hindered.

So every Spirit-filled believer should pray in tongues. However, not all will give divers tongues in public

Divers Kinds of Tongues and Interpretation of Tongues

meetings.

There is one scripture in the Bible which has been taken out of context. It is what Paul was saying in First Corinthians 12:30, *Have all the gifts of healing? do all speak with tongues? do all interpret?*

He was not asking the question, "Do all speak in tongues when they receive the Holy Spirit?" He was asking if everyone had a public ministry of divers kinds of tongues, because the next thing he said was, "Do all interpret?"

There can be no interpretation unless there is first an expression of a gift of divers kinds of tongues. When Paul was discussing this issue in verses 28-30, he was talking about ministry gifts, as well as spiritual gifts, that are given to the body of Christ. He was not talking about receiving the Holy Spirit. In verse 31, he said to covet the best gifts.

In a public meeting there must be order. When divers tongues come forth, most of the time it should be by the one in charge of the service, or someone in the congregation who is trained in the gifts and understands the moving of the Holy Spirit.

If someone stands up quickly and speaks out in tongues, interrupting the meeting, that is not order. God does not work in this way. If God gives you an utterance in divers tongues to deliver to the congregation, it will hold until the proper time. If you have a message in tongues, you should let the person in charge of the meeting know it. If you are acknowledged and given the floor, you have the right to bring forth the utterance in tongues.

However, there should be an interpretation of this message in tongues. If you are not acknowledged by the person in charge, you should hold your message until you are acknowledged. If not, you should not speak.

This has caused much confusion. Also, sometimes people have tongues for their own personal edification. They think it's a message in tongues, and they speak it out loud. They actually interrupt the service, and there will be interpretation.

Once I was having a New Year's Eve service. A man who is used in divers kinds of tongues was at the service. I asked him if he had a message. He stood to his feet and gave the message in tongues. I interpreted the message. He brought forth a second message, and by the Spirit, I interpreted again.

A young man came up to me looking very puzzled and said, "How could this be that you asked him if he had a message? I thought, if someone had a message, they would stand up and speak it out anytime they felt like it."

No, this is not true. If it is from God, it will hold until you get proper recognition to bring it forth. If you do not get the recognition, you should continue to hold it. The person in charge of the meeting, as I was, can sense the Spirit. They can have a person who is experienced in the gifts do this, as I did.

You can see how this keeps order. It is not to be spontaneous from the congregation; that would interrupt the service. God is a gentleman. He will not interrupt you.

If any man speak in an unknown tongue, let it be by two, or at the most by three, and that by course; and let one interpret. (1st Corinthians 14:27)

Divers Kinds of Tongues and Interpretation of Tongues

This really supports what I have just said. Paul said, let there be two or three in a public meeting give an utterance in tongues, and one interpret. This shows there should be order, not some stranger standing up with the utterance in tongues.

One who is acknowledged should give the tongue. He could interpret it, or it could be someone else. There could be wo or three; but the most who should participate would be three.

Paul was not talking about three messages in tongues and interpretation in a service. He was talking about the number of people who were involved in it.

It is possible that a meeting could go for some time with people being ministered to by prophecy or tongues and interpretation of tongues. It will exhort, edify, and encourage; and it will be in order.

You may go to a meeting where someone on the platform knows that he has an utterance in tongues, but does not have the interpretation. He will call on someone he knows, someone who is experienced in this gift of interpretation.

Also, there may be a tongue given, but no interpretation given. If the person in charge will have the tongue given again, he can bring forth the interpretation. There is no cause for confusion in any of the gifts of the Spirit when you have proper training and instruction.

Paul prayed in tongues a lot. He said,

18 I thank my God, I speak with tongues more than ye all:

19 Yet in the church I had rather speak five words with my understanding...than ten thou-

sand words in an unknown tongue. (1st Corinthians 14:18-19)

Why does he say that? Because with no interpretation, it would edify no one but himself. He knew not to just get up and speak in tongues without an interpretation.

13 Wherefore let him that speaketh in an unknown tongue pray that he may **interpret.**

14 For if I pray in an unknown tongue, my spirit prayeth, but my understanding is unfruitful.

15 What is it then? I will pray with the spirit, and I will pray with the understanding also: I will sing with the spirit, and I will sing with the understanding also. (1st Corinthians 14:13-15)

When you pray in tongues, you can pray for personal edification, to build yourself up, according to First Corinthians 14:4 and Jude 20. Romans 8:26 says you can pray with the help of the Spirit to make intercession for yourself and others. You can also pray in tongues and interpret your tongues (1st Corinthians 14:13). The next verse says, when you pray in tongues, your understanding is unfruitful.

You can interpret your tongue, then you can pray with the understanding of what you have prayed in tongues. If you have never interpreted your tongues before, I encourage you to do so. The next time you pray in tongues, stop and ask God for the interpretation.

Paul said he would sing in tongues and he would sing with his understanding. He is not talking about singing out of a song book. God will give you a song in your un-

Divers Kinds of Tongues and Interpretation of Tongues

derstanding after you have sung in tongues. It will be edifying, encouraging, and comforting to you. I do this in my prayer time sometimes.

Also, sometimes in a service there may be a few dozen, a few hundred, or several thousand singing in tongues. Most of the people there understand what is going on, and it is scriptural. Therefore, there is no harm done. All of these people are being blessed as they sing a melody in tongues in union with others.

However, it would make a difference if you went to a place where this was not common practice, or the people did not understand or believe in speaking in tongues. You would be out of order to sing in tongues there,, because it would cause confusion.

Sometimes with a husband and wife in the ministry, one will give the message in tongues and the other will interpret it. They may minister to the entire group as a whole. They may single people out for personal ministry. This is acceptable, as long as it is in order.

If they have a traveling ministry, they should have a local church which they support and are endorsed by. They may be pastors of a local church themselves.

If they are not faithful to a local church and are not endorsed by a pastor of integrity, then I would have nothing to do with them. The reason is, if they don't have a pastor, these people probably have a problem in submitting to a ministry. They can be prooting themselves, rather than meeting the needs of the people.

This type of ministry can get into the operation of other gifts, such as the gift of the word of knowledge, the word of wisdom, or the gifts of healing. So, if it is not a person who has the proper foundation, they can cause a lot of confusion and hurt.

I cannot say it enough; God does everything in order, and the gifts of the Spirit are for profit. So if you see this type of ministry occurring, make sure that it is not someone off in a prayer group who is rebelling against authority, or someone who is out doing their own thing in order to be recognized.

Remember this: the gifts of the Spirit will bring the body of Christ together and encourage them. They will not divide nor bring confusion. Those who are out of order or trying to do something without proper instruction will cause confusion--and God does not cause confusion.

How is it then, brethren? when ye come together, every one of you hath a psalm, hath a doctrine, hath a tongue, hath a revelation, hath an interpretation. (1st Corinthians 14:26)

Paul speaks here again on the order of the church. Different people may have something from the Lord, but there is a time and a place for all things. Paul is saying, what you have from the Lord may edify you, and you alone. It may not edify the church.

What is to be done publicly should edify the entire church. Just anyone should not be able to get up and speak. In verse 27, he said to let two, or three at the most. Here again, I remind you that all things must be cleared by the one who is in charge of the service. This will keep order in and confusion out.

This is why some people resort to holding meetings outside of their own church. They want to take a lot of time for special ministry. When they don't get to, they

Divers Kinds of Tongues and Interpretation of Tongues

establish a prayer group that is not under the authority of the church and pastor. Ultimately, they bring confusion and cause people to leave the church.

Now I realize some pastors say they believe in the supernatural gifts, but never permit them to be demonstrated in the church. This is a different case altogether.

Do not contest the authority of the pastor. Pray for him.

Can two walk together, except they be agreed? (Amos 3:3)

If you have prayed about the situation, given it time, spoken to the pastor about it, and he does not agree, then you should seek change. You should probably leave that church and find one you can be in agreement with. It would be better for you to leave quietly in love than gendering any strife.

Don't try to take anyone with you, either. When you can no longer agree with that pastor, you should not cause trouble.

If God is leading you into a public ministry, you will want to go, having been in one accord with your home church. You should prove yourself faithful and work where you are needed until God opens the door for you to step out into your own ministry.

If you are not faithful in the place where you are needed, don't expect other doors to be opened for you. This is true, no matter how proficient you are in the spiritual gifts.

The nine gifts of the Spirit have been given to the body of Christ for one main reason. That is for the demonstration of God's power to be brought to deal with everyday situations and problems, both to believers and non-believers. These gifts cannot be conjured up as you think necessary, but are given as God wills for a specific time and purpose.

An ardent desire with pure motives will cause you to be the sensitive individual God desires for use in the gifts. As you continue into the study of the ministry gifts, you will see how they work together to affect positive change in the body of Christ.

Chapter 21

THE MINISTRY GIFTS

11 And he gave some, apostles; and some, prophets; some, evangelists; and some, pastors and teachers;

12 For the perfecting of the saints, for the work of the ministry, for the edifying of the body of Christ:

13 Till we all come in the unity of the faith, and of the knowledge of the Son of God, unto a perfect man, unto the measure of the stature of the fulness of Christ:

14 That we henceforth be not more children, tossed to and fro, and carried about with every wind of doctrine, by the sleight of men, and cunning craftiness, whereby they lie in wait to deceive;

15 But speaking the truth in love, may grow up into him in all things, which is the head, even

Christ. (Ephesians 4:11-15)

When Jesus was on earth, he actually fulfilled every office of the ministry. But when He returned to the Father, He gave these gifts to men for the completion of the work He had begun.

The ministry gifts are different from the nine spiritual gifts that we have examined in the previous chapters.

However, the ministry gifts do go hand-in-hand with the spiritual gifts. You do not have to be called into one of the five ministry offices in order to have the nine spiritual gifts operating through you. If you have an office within the five ministries, you will have several gifts operating in your life.

The five ministry gifts are given to lead the body of Christ, to bring maturity, and to fully equip the saints for the work of the ministry and the building up of the body of Christ. The result should be that the body is no longer like a little child, changing its mind every time it hears another doctrine. It should be a mature body which learns to walk in love.

The five different offices that have been given to the body of Christ are still God's plan. These ministries have not been taken away. Great men such as the apostles Paul and Peter have died and gone to be with Jesus, but the office is still here for men to fill, doing the work of Jesus Christ.

In this twentieth century, people readily accept the title of the pastor, teacher, and evangelist. But not many readily accept the apostle and the prophet. Many will tell you that the prophet's ministry was for the people in the Old Testament, and the apostle was for the New

Testament.

Thus they really have not accepted the **purpose and position** of the pastor, teacher, and evangelist that are given to us by God. These five ministries all work together, in love, with respect for each other. Each of them complement the other's work. These five are given the direction for the body of Christ; not just one man, nor one office, but all together.

The purpose of the five ministry gifts is in some respects the same as that of the nine spiritual gifts. They are: to help bring encouragement, to reveal to the body of Christ how to come into unity, and to aid its growth to maturity.

These offices of ministry are gifts given by God. You can neither decide that you want to be one, and put on the title, nor can you go to school and learn how to be one.

God must call you first. You can then to to school, prepare, and study to show yourself approved.

There must be that time of preparation, although preparation alone does not qualify you. It takes the call, preparation, prayer, and real compassion.

The process of maturing in one of the ministry gifts is much the same as that of a child maturing in the areas of life. They learn may facts from school and from their parents, but the real growth takes place in their interaction with others.

You may study and go to Bible school (which I recommend), but the real task begins in the field itself. After you begin, it takes from five to seven years to develop the office and to gain the respect of the office to which you are called.

There are people today with a title who are very sincere, but they have no fruit of the particular office they occupy.

One reason may be that they are not called to that particular office. I don't say this to be critical or judgmental, but it is a matter of fact that some people go through their entire life never knowing what they are called to do.

There are people who have one of the titles of the five ministry gifts, mean well, and want to work for God, but should really be in the ministry of helps, working under someone who is chosen and qualified. Being where God wants you to be should be the most important thing to you, not seeking the attention and applause of men.

What difference does it make if God calls you to the ministry of helps and you serve under another authority? Your reward will be just as great. There is a great need for people to work in the ministry of helps, serving, and not seeking their own, but seeking the kingdom of God and helping to meet the needs of hurting people in this world.

One of the best ways for a person to start in the ministry is to attach himself to one that is successful and serve there faithfully until it's time to move out. You will learn a great deal by being close to the anointing of that person. The secret is to serve faithfully, not just waiting for the day you will get to minister.

Instead, do all you do with love, both for God and that ministry (1st Corinthians 16:14). If you are not faithful serving under another's ministry, or you are not doing it with the right motives, you must ask yourself the following question. When you do get into your own ministry, what kind of people do you want serving you?

I want to share a word of advice to the one who serves:

22 Servants, obey in all things your masters according to the flesh; not with eyeservice, as menpleasers; but in singleness of heart, fearing God:

23 And whatsoever ye do, do it heartily, as to the Lord, and not unto men;

24 Knowing that of the Lord ye shall receive the reward of the inheritance: for ye serve the Lord Christ. (Colossians 3:22-24)

This is very clear about motives. If you are doing something in order to please men or score points, it has been done in vain. You must not serve for the recognition of man, but for the Lord. In doing so, you will not expect everything to come from the one you serve. Your rewards will come from God.

There is also responsibility for the ones being served. They should operate in love and not take advantage of those who serve under them.

Masters, give unto your servants that which is just and equal; knowing that ye also have a Master in heaven. (Colossians 4:1)

The one being served will treat those around him in the same manner that he desires to be treated. I really believe that serving is a great opportunity for one desiring to develop into one of the five ministry gifts.

The one that is serving will be able to see many things first-hand without having the total responsibility. He can obtain invaluable experience. When he is in his own ministry, he will have greater insight of how to deal with it.

I am not saying that this is the way it should be in every case, because there are some people who don't need this "internship." The bottom line though, is to be led of the Lord, follow Him, and He will direct you in the path that you should follow.

Many people are called into a full-time ministry, but do not have to hold an office of the five ministry gifts. An example of this would be the office of the psalmist, which is very important to the body of Christ. This office should be respected and given its proper place, but there has been some confusion and hurt in this area.

There have been those who have been professional entertainers in the world and they have accepted Jesus as their Savior. Because they are well known, they are given an open door to minister. However, all this person has is his testimony, which, by itself, is not a qualification to lead. Many times, though, he is put into a place of authority with no real foundation. Because he has assumed a place of leadership, certain qualifications are expected from him by the congregation and the pastor. When mistakes are made, it causes hurt and confusion, and real harm can be done.

I believe everyone should be taught the Word first and should be submitted to a local ministry. This will qualify them and teach them how to walk in faith. They should not go out expecting only the church to meet their needs.

Don't misunderstand me. I know that a workman is worthy of his hire. But when he knows that God is his

The Ministry Gifts

source, and he has learned some real Christian principles under a godly man, his needs will be met when he goes out to minister. This keeps out confusion and frustration on both the one doing the ministering and the one being ministered to.

I believe the ministry of the psalmist should be well taken care of financially by the local church. However, that should not be the reason they are ministering there. If a person is in the ministry of a psalmist, and doesn't learn to be submitted and taught, he will always have problems in the ministry. All who minister must minister by the Spirit of Christ. If it is not done in love, once again, it will be only a religious noise.

Many in the church do not understand the psalmist's ministry. When a music minister comes and brings their own equipment, there should not be strife as a result. Each should have an understanding of what is expected from the other before the meeting is arranged. Neither should have demands placed upon them that would cause the other to be put in an inferior position. There should be joy in the meetings, not tension and pressure. I long to see us all work together, not everyone just doing "their own thing."

We should all be humble servants who are working for the same purpose and goal: that of bringing Jesus back for His children. There should be no haughtiness, but meekness and gentleness in character.

There are those who attend Bible school and see others who have gone out from school, started a church or ministry, and have been successful. These people go out and attempt to duplicate what others have done. But that doesn't work. This causes them to be discouraged. There are also times when a person's ministry is successful in the beginning, but at some point, no longer fulfills their expectations or goals.

By being the leader of the congregation or other ministry, there is always the underlying pressure that he should have the answers to every problem. This is not the time to let fear of losing the position, or pride interfere with the accomplishment of the God-inspired vision. He should confide in and obtain encouragement from someone more experienced in the ministry. **Withdrawing and refusing to face the problem only causes distrust and confusion among those under him.**

Being in Bible school for one or two years and hearing the Word is enough to excite anyone so much that they would want to take a city. However, remember that you must be in your proper place to be effective. If you are not, it won't work.

Some have come out of a Bible school, received a mandate from God in the form of a rhema word about a particular city or certain type of ministry, and it grows to be a large ministry, seemingly overnight. I thank God for this, but it does not happen this way for everyone.

The person who goes out and does not obtain the same result should not get under any kind of bondage because their ministry is not of the same magnitude as someone else's. **Only compare what your ministry is doing by what God has told you to do.**

Also, there are those who do not get a mandate for a particular city. They just act on the Word.

15 And he said unto them, Go ye into all the world, and preach the gospel to every creature.

16 He that believeth and is baptized shall be saved; but he that believeth not shall be damned.

17 And these signs shall follow them that believe; In my name shall they cast out devils; they shall speak with new tongues;

18 They shall take up serpents; and if they drink any deadly thing, it shall not hurt them; they shall lay hands on the sick, and they shall recover. (Mark 16:15-18)

Sometimes these ministries are successful. Sometimes they aren't. Whatever the case, you should always go for a specific purpose--to meet a need. Never just go to have your needs met. Sharon and I have made it and have come through some obstacles, but there was a time in my evangelistic ministry when all I wanted to do was preach. I lived, breathed, and ate the ministry. I loved it, even though it kept me away from my family the majority of the time. Our children were small, and Sharon was home alone with them, which put a great strain on all of us. One day God spoke to me and told me to come aside for a while.

He talked with me and gave me an overall look at my family and my ministry. He gave me a vision for the city where I now live, and showed me the way to align my motives with the Word of God. Things changed for me, my wife, and my children.

I believe the following priorities should be for everyone, both in the ministry or for the laity:

1. Your personal relationship with God.

2. Your personal relationship with your mate.
3. Your personal relationship with your children.
4. Your personal relationship with your church.
5. Your mission, job, or ministry.

I have always been an effective minister. However, since all of my priorities are now straight, I enjoy all areas of life. I don't spend all of my time just in the ministry. My wife and I have quality time. My children and I have quality time. These things are so important.

There has seemingly been a gap between the laity and the ministry--both trying to understand each other, and both sometimes becoming frustrated. When Cod calls or chooses a person for one of the offices of the fivefold ministry, He gives that gift to that person. That person then assumes responsibilities which the lay person does not have. Sometimes it puts a gap between the two. It should not be this way. This ministry is a gift to the body. It should be treated as such.

It's time for God's people to understand that there is a difference between submission and total surrender. You should never give your will to any man. Give it only to God.

Be ye followers of me, even as I also am of Christ. (1st Corinthians 11:1)

God has given us leaders who are examples of the Christian faith and demonstrate God's power. Follow the faith of God, but never that which is contrary to the Word of God.

Keep this in mind, and there will never be a need to look back on a situation with regret.

The Ministry Gifts

Paul said to follow him as he followed Christ. He made it very plain that the responsibility was to follow him only as he followed Christ. There have been those who supposedly were men of God, but erred from the truth because men began to praise them.

They took their eyes off God, became puffed up, and got into strange doctrine. They would take advantage of those who would allow them to do so.

Then there are those who are nothing more than wolves in sheep's clothing. They are only out for selfish gain. They are not looking into the Word and following the voice of the Spirit. This causes people to become wounded spiritually and lose respect for the ministry.

Some have problems submitting to the ministry gifts. Just because there have been those who have been nothing more than charlatans and have hurt people and taken advantage of people, this does not change the Word of God.

Wherefore hs saith, When he ascended up on high, he led captivity captive, and gave gifts unto men. (Ephesians 4:8)

Jesus gave the gifts to men: apostles, prophets, evangelists, pastors, and teachers to bring you to maturity, to build you up, to teach you to love one another, to work together, and to respect each other (v. 11).

Those who hold the offices of the five ministry gifts will have great respect for one another, help each other, and work together. They will all be promoters of unity and be servers. They will tend to the needs of the people through having the heart of a servant.

Chapter 22

THE MINISTRY OF AN APOSTLE

And God hath set some in the church, first apostles. (1st Corinthians 12:28)

Paul said that God has set some in the church, first apostles. The apostle's ministry is very important. His ministry was mentioned by Paul as being first, because at times he must function in all of the other four ministry offices.

The word apostle from First Corinthians 12:28 means an ambassador of the gospel. An ambassador is the highest ranking diplomatic representative appointed by one country or government to represent it in another. He is an official messenger or agent with a special mission.

The apostle is sent from God to his people with a special mission. He is officially a commissioner of Christ with miraculous power. One of the reasons he is said to have miraculous power is because of the gifts of the Spirit that operate through his ministry. The apostle is sent to do the job that Jesus would do if He went Himself.

Very few people have really understood the apostle's ministry or authority. He has God's character, and he understands the needs of the people. He is bold. The apostle will go into an area, break up the fallow ground, and sow the seeds of righteousness. He will stay there until fruit is produced from his labor.

There are times when he goes in and begins a new work at the time he is the prophet to that local group. He has a vision for the church. By the word of wisdom he has the direction of whether to be just a local church or to take a city.

He also stands in the office of a pastor. He stays near them, shows them much care, leads, and protects them.

The apostle will also teach the word of faith to keep them balanced and walking in love.

Then there are times when he has to stir up the flock, which is part of the ministry of an evangelist.

> *Whereunto I am appointed a preacher, and an apostle, and a teacher of the Gentiles.* (2nd Timothy 1:11)

This bears out the fact that the ministry of the apostle is diverse. He is able to help in any aspect of the work of the church.

This does not mean that he will cut himself off from the other ministries and attempt to do everything himself. No, he will be submissive to other men of God and have great respect for them. What God reveals to him will be in agreement with what God is giving to other ministries in the body of Christ.

> *15 But when it pleased God, who separated me from my mother's womb, and called me by his grace,*
>
> *16 To reveal his Son in me, that I might preach him among the heathen; immediately I conferred not with flesh and blood:*
>
> *17 Neither went I up to Jerusalem to them which were apostles before me; but I went into Arabia, and returned again unto Damascus.*
>
> *18 Then after three years I went up to Jerusalem to see Peter, and abode with him fifteen days.* (Galatians 1:15-18)

Paul explains here how God called him to be an apostle and to preach to the heathen. He did not confer with men at the beginning of his ministry. But after three years, he spent fifteen days with Peter. I'm sure he was sharing with Peter the revelations which he had received.

Galatians Two says, after fourteen years, Paul went back to Jerusalem. By revelation, God told him to go and talk privately with other leaders of the church.

He shared with them what he had been teaching, and it was in agreement with what the other apostles were teaching.

James, Cephas, and John appeared to be men of great importance and supporters of his ministry. They saw Paul as a real apostle of God. They gave him and Barnabas the

The Power Of God's Character

right hand of fellowship, which was a mark of confidence and friendship among the Jews.

They added only one thing to Paul's teaching--that he would remember the poor. Paul was always eager to do this.

The apostle's ministry will stand out because of this boldness. He may be sent into an area with the word of correction. Paul brought correction in Galatians Two. The Jewish legalists were saying that circumcision was necessary for salvation, which caused Peter to become fearful and withdraw from the Gentiles.

He had also been fellowshipping with them, but he stopped. There were other Jewish Christians who followed Peter's example, even though they knew better.

When Paul heard about this situation, he told Peter,

"If thou, being a Jew, livest after the manner of Gentiles, and not as do the Jews, why compellest thou the Gentiles to live as do the Jews?"
(Galatians 2:14)

Paul spoke publicly with boldness to Peter and to the other Christians. Order was restored because of his correction.

The apostle's ministry has not changed since the days of the early church. It still has the same authority. In this particular place, God used Paul for a local situation.

I believe it would be the same today. An apostle could bring correction to a local church or group, if something was out of order.

If someone's actions caused confusion in an area of ministry, or if they had not shown courtesy to other min-

The Ministry of an Apostle

istries, an apostle could bring correction to them. The one bringing the correction would have to have the authority, plus the respect of other ministers in the area.

When someone is spoken to and corrected, whether the correction is about a personal problem in life, their character is not in line with the Word, they are teaching false doctrine, or they are causing confusion by unethical practices, if they do not heed it, the matter should be brought before several of the men in the area. They should then speak with him. If he does not heed, Paul said that he should be marked.

Now I beseech you, brethren, mark them which cause divisions and offences contrary to the doctrine which ye have learned; and avoid them. (Romans 16:17)

If it appears error has come into the body of Christ by false teaching, one man could not stand up on nationwide television and correct the entire body. It would take a number of men who are walking in the apostle's ministry to bring the correction needed.

No **one** man has been given the authority or right to bring balance to the body of Christ. When greater revelation is being brought to the body of Christ, it will be in line with the Word of God. Other seasoned men and women of God will also be speaking and saying the same thing.

In the New Testament, the apostles were very bold. There were times when they would teach and minister to the sick and people would be healed. The authorities would feel intimidated and tell them not to teach and heal in the name of Jesus anymore. However, they would al-

The Power Of God's Character

ways do what God had told them to do.

On one occasion, Peter and John had prayed for a lame man, and he was healed--causing quite a stir among the people. They had been threatened and told not to teach in the name of Jesus any more.

19 But Peter and John answered and said unto them, Whether it be right in the sight of God to hearken unto you more than unto God, judge ye.

20 For we cannot but speak the things which we have seen and heard. (Acts 4:19-20)

At times their boldness would cause them to be sent to jail, but it did not stop them from doing what they believed in. I believe it should be the same today.

The apostle is not only bold, but he has another side as well. He is loving, and cares for people, especially for those called into the ministry.

He has a desire to teach and train them for service in the kingdom of God. Paul took special interest in Timothy and trained him for the ministry. Paul shared many valuable treasures of the ministry with him.

Holding faith, and a good conscience; which some having put away concerning faith have made shipwreck. (1st Timothy 1:19)

Paul was telling Timothy to walk in his own faith, not to do what he had seen others do. If he had done what God had told him, he would not have become shipwrecked. His faith would have worked for him.

Paul also taught Timothy about character.

Let no man despise thy youth; but be thou an example of the believers, in word and in con-

versation, in charity, in spirit, in faith, in purity. (1st Timothy 4:12)

Paul told Timothy that as a leader, he must demonstrate the character of Christ.

You are to be an example of what is right in your daily life. You cannot tell someone what is expected of them, and not live up to it yourself. More is expected of a leader.

I believe some of our Bible schools have been started with real vision and compassion. The founders usually have a burning desire to teach and train men and women, not only in doctrine, but also in character and true Christian principles, and how to do the work of the ministry.

They see the need to evangelize the world. Through the sharing of their experiences and personal teaching, they look to help people become successful more quickly. I believe it is the desire of a genuine apostle to equip, train, educate, and ordain young people for service in the ministry.

Paul called himself an apostle, laid hands on people, and ordained them for the ministry.

And when they had ordained them elders in every church, and had prayed with fasting, they commended them to the Lord, on whom the believed. (Acts 14:23)

The apostles in this day will ordain and encourage new ministries, help guide them to maturity, and will not put pressure on them to be fully developed when they first begin their ministry.

Some come out of Bible School with a direct mandate from God about their ministry, while others don't seem to have any direction at all concerning what God wants them to do. It is very important for those who have received no distinct direction to join themselves up with an established ministry and work there until God gives them direction, or until they receive enough experience to go out on their own.

Satan will try to stop anyone holding an office within the five ministries, if he is doing the work of God with a specific direction. Paul said in Second Corinthians Twelve that a messenger of Satan was sent to buffet him. It was not sent from God, Satan sent it. Satan is not sent by God. He comes to us at his own will as a roaring lion, seeking whom he may devour.

He does this to direct your attention from your purpose and call. You should settle this fact before you get started in your ministry. If you don't, you won't stand when he begins to attack you.

You will criticized by one and applauded by another. Neither one should have an effect on you. Your strength and security should come from the power of God.

To be an apostle of God, you must be called. It is not a ministry that you decide you want. God chooses you for this specific ministry.

Paul, an apostle, (not of men, neither by man, but by Jesus Christ, and God the Father, who raised him from the dead;) (Galatians 1:1)

Paul was saying that God called him to be an apostle. Man did not appoint him, call him, or give him a prophecy for this ministry. It was God's divine purpose for him.

In the beginning of this chapter, I said an apostle may be used of God in all areas of ministry. His ministry is diversified, but he is never to try to fill all of the offices. Only when there is a particular area of need will he be chosen to fill one of the other offices. This will only be for a season.

The apostle is compared to the thumb of the hand. Because he can touch all the other fingers, he has a primary unction. He can touch all the other areas of ministry when needed.

God has four more ministry gifts, and they all have their place in the body of Christ. Jesus was an apostle **to us** when He was here. Now He is an apostle **for us.** He was sent from the Father to us, and then He returned to the Father to intercede for us.

Remember that the definition of an apostle is one who is sent.

Chapter 23

THE MINISTRY OF THE PROPHET

And he gave some, apostles; and some, prophets;... (Ephesians 4:11)

The ministry of a prophet publicly declares that which cannot be known by natural means. He is a "seer." He reveals the past, the present, and the future.

The office is one that is called by God. God does the choosing. You can't just decide that this is the ministry for you and begin training for it.

Paul said that God gave the gift of ministry of a prophet to some, not all. First Corinthians 14:31 says that all may prophesy, but all are not prophets.

There is a difference. He that prophesies by the gift of prophecy brings edification, exhortation, and comfort. The prophet will give revelation. It takes several of the

The Power Of God's Character

gifts of the Spirit to make the ministry of the prophet complete. The gift of the word of knowledge is to reveal the past and present. The gift of the word of wisdom is to reveal the future. The gift of discerning of spirits is to look into the realm of the spirit world. And then there is the gift of prophecy.

The prophet does not have to deliver his revelation with prophecy. He can just speak the message.

The prophet was more noticed in the Old Testament than in the New Testament, because the people were not born again. Their communication with God was only through a prophet or a priest.

The prophet would always bring a word of God to the people. Sometimes the message from God was to destroy the city. If the people believed the prophet and repented, God spared them from the promised judgment.

Other times, there would be a word given about famine or drought that would take place for a certain amount of time. God would always sustain his people during the time of drought.

There would be prophets sent to different individuals for different reasons. Sometimes prophets would be sent to tell people that they were going to die, and other times, to warn them of danger. Sometimes prophets anointed certain ones to be King.

Throughout the Old Testament we see how the prophet had great insight and was mightily used of God. It was a prophet who told of the birth of Jesus. He also prophesied of how He must die and give His life for you and me.

The prophet prophesied of the new birth.

Their ministry has not vanished. God still has prophets today.

And he gave some,... prophets. (Ephesians 4:11)

If they were not to be a part of the church, then Paul would have stated it. Instead, he said that God put them in the church to bring maturity to the body of Christ.

Jesus came and redeemed us from spiritual death and gave us life. We now have God's anointing upon us, since we are born again and spirit-filled. We can talk to God through Jesus Christ. We have the Holy Spirit to help, comfort and lead us in our day-to-day life. We also have the Word of God to look to for guidance.

As a result, under the new covenant, there is not the same demand for a prophet as there was under the old covenant. You should know God for yourself and be able to hear what God is saying to you about your personal life.

You should be spiritually tuned in to hear, when God is using a prophet to bring direction to the body of Christ.

Surely the Lord God will do nothing but he revealeth his secret unto his servants the prophets. (Amos 3:7)

Even though this is an Old Testament scripture, when God reveals greater truth to the body of Christ, it will be done through the ministry of the apostles and prophets.

Ephesians 4:11-12 says God put the ministries in the church for the saints. The saints, the body, are not to lead or direct the ministry.

I am not saying that God will not give you revelation. If you are born again and spirit-filled, He will, if you ask for it.

The direction for the church comes through the ministry of the apostles and prophets. The apostles and prophets are ordinary people whom God calls. He chooses them for this special work.

They are not different, but they have been given a gift from God. A very special anointing which a lay person does not have is upon these ministries.

It is important that you understand this and give proper respect and honor to the ministry gifts. It is not the person that you are honoring, it is the gift. God uses whomever He chooses.

You and I may not have chosen the one God did, but God looks on the heart. He knows what He is doing, and I trust Him. I have no problem knowing the ministry gifts which God has given to the body of Christ.

The apostles and prophets reveal truth to the body of Christ. They keep the church on its proper course, and keep it pointed in the right direction.

There are times when people get off track and speak accordingly, but the ministry of the prophet has insight by this supernatural gift that you can trust. What he says will always be in line with the Word of God.

> *...that utterance may be given unto me, that I may open my mouth boldly, to make known the mystery of the gospel.* (Ephesians 6:19)

The word "mystery" in this verse also means secret. God tells His secrets to the apostles and the prophets, for them to be unveiled at the proper time. They speak the mind of God with boldness.

The Ministry of a Prophet

The message that they proclaim cannot be by natural means; it is a supernatural utterance. When God uses a prophet to speak, he will be recognized and respected by other prophets, apostles, pastors, and teachers as having the position to bring direction to the body of Christ.

He will also submit to other prophets and ministries. He will allow them to judge his prophecies to see if he has spoken by true revelation, or from his own spirit.

God matures men along with the ministry. If their ministry has not been proven over and over again, weigh closely what is said by them.

God opens the door, and other seasoned men judge what they are saying. As they gain respect, they can be trusted more. However, don't ever trust any man over your Bible.

Let the prophets speak two or three, and let the other judge. (1st Corinthians 14:29)

If a man claims to be a prophet and will not submit himself to other men of God who have approved ministries, I personally would not want anything to do with his ministry.

This has happened so many times. God has used a man by giving him a message for a certain time and place. People would get their eyes on the man, and he would take the credit and glory, instead of giving it to God. He becomes puffed up with himself and filled with pride. The door is then opened for error. He separates himself from other men of God for the reason of not wanting to be corrected. He will not submit, and he becomes deceived and gives himself over to false doctrine.

In the fifth chapter of Acts, people sold their possessions and gave the money to the apostles to distribute as needed. This was for a specific time, place and purpose.

We have not been told in the scriptures to duplicate this practice. "So-called" prophets have prophesied to do this, and it has been tried over and over again. Shy away from those who are telling you to live commune style.

I believe that God wants His people to live everywhere, not hidden away in a mountain, or off somewhere all by themselves.

> *Let your light so shine before men, that they may see your good works, and glorify your Father which is in heaven.* (Matthew 5:16)

If you go off and hide in a corner to serve God, your works would not be seen and observed by the world. You would not be able to witness to them and show them love and kindness. God wouldn't be glorified by your good works, either.

Beware of those who would lead you away from the body of Christ and isolate you and have you wait there until Jesus comes. Beware of those who compel you to stay somewhere through hard and rough times. This is contradicting the scriptures. This will put you into a position of following man, not God. Never forget what Paul said,

> *Be ye followers of me, even as I also am of Christ.* (1st Corinthians 11:1)

Much harm has been done because men have led people off and prophesied for them to store up food for hard times. This is not God at all. God is our provider. He is more than enough.

God is our refuge and strength, a very present help in trouble. (Psalm 46:1)

God opened the Red Sea for Moses and the children of Israel. He gave them manna from heaven. He even gave the children of Israel flesh when they asked for it. Jesus took five loaves of bread and two fish and multiplied it for a multitude.

Neither God nor His power have changed. He will make provision for you. Don't be deceived by those who use scare tactics. Keep in mind that everything they do is motivated by fear.

For God hath not given us the spirit of fear; but of power, and of love, and of a sound mind. (2nd Timothy 1:7)

You should never make a move out of fear. All of your moves should be made by faith in God. God will always provide and protect you wherever you are. Don't listen to anyone who would cause you confusion.

4 And when he putteth forth his own sheep, he goeth before them, **and the sheep follow him: for they know his voice.**

5 And a stranger will they not follow, *but will flee from him: for they know not the voice of strangers.* (John 10:4-5)

Don't listen to a voice that is strange and does not line up with the Word of God. According to the twenty-third Psalm, a real prophet of God will lead the people of God into safety and peace. He will show them where there is green pastures. He tells them to fear no evil, because God is with them.

Jeremiah twenty-three tells of judgments that will be upon men who have taken advantage of people with no real foundation, so that when false prophets speak, they are swayed by the "prophet's" words.

There are people living in fear today because of this kind of man. Some have even hardened their hearts against God because of what they have heard.

but the prophet, which shall presume to speak a word in my name, which I have not commanded him to speak, or that shall speak in the name of other gods, even that prophet shall die. (Deuteronomy 18:20)

It is very dangerous for a man to say that he is speaking a word from God when he is not.

Beware of those who prophesy doom and gloom. Jesus has come to us and given us hope. The Bible says in John 10:10 that Jesus has come so that we can have life and have it more abundantly--here and now, not just when we get to heaven. There is enough doom and gloom going on in the world, so who wants to go to church to hear it? Who want to turn the radio or television on and hear it by a so called prophet of God?

God is telling us through His prophets how to change the world, not how to be overcome by it. God does not leave us hopeless or helpless, He tells us what to do.

In Second Kings, the eighth chapter, Elisha had prophesied of a famine that would last for seven years. There was a woman there whose son he had raised from the dead. He told her to take her family to some other country where there was provision. She took her family to the land of the Philistines for the duration of the famine. After it was over, she returned to the land of Israel to find that her property had been illegally occupied.

She then went to see the king about getting her house and land back. When she went in, Elisha's servant was talking with the king and telling him how Elisha had raised a boy from the dead. He noticed her and said to the king,

"This is the mother of the boy that I was telling you about."

The king asked her if it was the truth, and she told him that it was. Then the king directed one of his officials to see to it that everything that she owned was restored to her, plus the value of any crops that had been harvested during her absence.

God used a prophet to help this woman. She was given direction to get back what was hers, and what she had lost. I believe that the prophet's ministry is doing the same today.

In Acts, the eleventh chapter, some prophets came from Jerusalem to Antioch. One of them, Agabus, prophesied that there would be a famine. It happened during the reign of Claudius. So the believers sent relief to the Christians in Judea. Each gave as much as they could.

Apparently the famine was not in the whole world. If so, they would have sent relief to others beside Judea. God revealed the future to the prophets and told the people what to do. The people followed the prophets' instructions, and the needs where met.

The prophet is a "seer." You could say that he is the eyes of the church. He will always help and bring hope to the body of Christ.

Prophets will point us in the right direction to receive the blessings of God and to be restored from the things that Satan has stolen from us. This provision from God will meet our needs and supply more than enough to help publish the gospel into all the world.

Don't be disturbed by the false prophets that are prophesying doom and gloom. Time is short. Hear what the Spirit of God has to say. He will lead you into victory.

Chapter 24

THE MINISTRY OF THE EVANGELIST

And he gave some, apostles; and some, prophets; and some, evangelists:... (Ephesians 4:11)

The ministry of the evangelist is one of the five ministry gifts which God has placed in the church. All gifts are given by God. You cannot choose to be an evangelist; God chooses you.

Some people identify the gift of the evangelist as one who travels. This may be true. However, many people can travel and minister and never be called or chosed for that office.

One who is called and chosen for this ministry gift will be a proclaimer of the gospel, good news and righteousness. He will stand out from the one who is only an exhorter.

He will in many cases be a preacher, not a teacher. Teaching instructs. Inspired preaching produces the enthusiasm that is needed to act on what you have heard.

In these latter days, we have noticed more teachers in the body of Christ. However, if you are a preacher, and you know that is what you are called to be, don't try to suppress it or conform to someone else's idea that preaching is not the "in" thing.

Preachers are a part of the ministry, and evangelists will preach. Don't be an imitator. Be yourself. Be original. God will give you creativity in your ministry. If you are trying to act and sound like others in order to be accepted, the truth is that you will never be accepted.

In the sixth chapter of Acts, there were several deacons appointed by the apostles. They were men of good report, honest, and full of the Holy Ghost. Hands were laid upon these men by the apostles. Philip was one of these men.

He became an evangelist, but he started his ministry by serving and being a deacon. When he was appointed to be a deacon he may have known that he was called to be an evangelist, but he served there, because it was an open door. He may have felt that was the extent of his ministry, but nevertheless, he was appointed as a deacon. Later we see him doing the work of an evangelist and being addressed by others as holding that office.

5 Then Philip went down to the city of Samaria, and preached Christ unto them.

6 And the people with one accord gave heed unto those things which Philip spake, hearing and seeing the miracles which he did.

7 For unclean spirits, crying with loud voice, came out of many that were possessed with them: and many taken with palsies, and that were lame, were healed.

8 And there was great joy in that city. (Acts 8:5-8)

In this passage of scripture I see several things that pertain to the ministry of an evangelist. He preaches Christ, and souls are saved as a result. As Philip preached Christ, the Bible says that the people gave need to what he said with one accord, and received Jesus. Crowds gathered to hear his message.

The gift of the evangelist is special and unique. It draws people to hear, even without advertisement, because of the demonstration of God's power. I see the power gifts at work in the ministry of Philip. People who were lame and paralyzed were healed--which was the gift of healing at work.

He cast out demon spirits through the gift of faith. The scripture said they saw the miracles which Philip did. They could have been calling a healing a miracle, or miraculous things which were not recorded could have taken place.

There was great joy in that city. The message and ministry of the evangelist will bring joy because of the good news and the healings that take place.

When you compare the ministry to a hand, the middle finger represents the evangelist. He is between the prophet and the pastor. The evangelist works closely with the prophet, who sees the future, and the pastor who is the shepherd.

When the church sometimes becomes complacent, the ministry of the evangelist stands out and brings to the church just what it needs to change that condition.

Remember that the ministry of the evangelist always complements that of a pastor. He does not divide the church or steal the allegiance of the people from the pastor. He directs the people to the pastor and supports him.

He will not come to a church or city seeking support for himself and his ministry. He will instead consider the local church and the pastor. He will point the people who receive Christ, and the believers without a church home who are stirred, to a local church where the uncompromised truth is taught. He will not use the reputation of the pastor to become well-known, then tell the people to come back, as he is holding his own meeting immediately thereafter.

This causes confusion, and God does not cause confusion. It also causes strife and division within the five ministries. According to the scripture, the five ministries are to be promoters of unity and maturity, not of division.

The evangelist's ministry prepares the way for churches to be started. Many times, he goes where there is no church and sows the seed to the uncompromised Word.

A pastor will then come in behind him and open a church. In Acts, the eighth chapter, Philip went and preached Christ to prepare the way. The apostles then sent Peter and John after him. That is one reason why, in some cities, churches seem to grow by leaps and bounds.

Many times it is because there have been seeds sown there for years, and others are reaping the harvest of these seeds.

The evangelist will sometimes do personal work. Such an example is found in Acts, chapter eight, where the angel of the Lord told Philip to go to the road that runs from Jerusalem through the Gaza desert.

Philip did, and there was a eunuch of great authority under Candice, the Queen. He was riding in his chariot and reading from the prophet Isaiah.

Then Philip, being led by the Spirit, joined himself to the chariot. He asked the man, who was reading, if he understood what he was reading. The man answered,

"How can I, when there is no one to instruct me?"

Philip began to explain this passage of scripture to him. The eunuch believed, then accepted Jesus Christ as his Lord and Savior. They came to the Jordan river and Philip baptized him.

The Spirit of God then translated Philip to another place. This translation was another example of the gift of working of miracles.

My ministry started out very small. However, I stayed faithful to God. I can remember, many times, going to a city to preach in a local church, or sometimes I would preach in a tent. Hardly anyone knew me. I prayed and preached to the small crowds--sometimes only a dozen or two, but the power of God was manifested. People got saved, and healings took place. The crowds would grow and the church or tent would be filled after several days. Sometimes I would stay in one place for five or six weeks. Then I saw proof of my labor, and it was worth all the effort. God continued to use me across the United States, and in other countries. He gave me favor with other min-

The Power Of God's Character

istries and continued to open doors for me. If you make an effort, you don't have to ask or beg for a place to minister. Your gift will make room for you.

The five ministry gifts should be prayed for by the saints. There should be continuous intercession, because these ministries are on the front lines. Also, other ministries should spend time in intercession praying for one another.

In any one of these offices, there are afflictions and persecutions which must be endured. Satan is always out trying to hinder any ministry. When he does, he hinders others from receiving.

Paul, addressing Timothy as an evangelist, said,

But watch thou in all things, endure afflictions, do the work of an evangelist, make full proof of thy ministry. (2nd Timothy 4:5)

The word "afflictions" here does not mean sickness, or even suggest it. It means to undergo hardship or suffer trouble.

I do not mean this to sound negative at all. It is true that if you step out for God, it must be a quality decision, and you must know that you are called. Satan will try your faith to see if you mean business.

Chapter 25

THE MINISTRY OF A PASTOR

And he gave some, apostles; and some, prophets; and some, evangelists; and some, pastors... (Ephesians 4:11)

The ministry of the pastor, like the other four ministries, is an office given only by God. God calls and appoints people to this position. One may go to Bible School and spend much time studying and preparing to be a pastor. If God has not called them for the office of a pastor, they will never be one. Even though they may have a church and have the title, that still does not make them a pastor.

God gives the pastor a heart for the people. You either have it or you don't.

In Ephesians four we find the only place the word "pastor" is used in the New Testament. It comes from the

Greek word "poimen", and it is the same word from which "shepherd" is derived. So you can say that a pastor is a shepherd.

A shepherd remains close to his flock and shows a great amount of care for them. When a comparison to the hand is made, the pastor's position is the ring finger. He is married to his flock. The pastor is compassionate, loving, kind, and understanding. He is always protecting the flock from danger. He watches over them, keeping them together. He guards them against false doctrines.

One must have certain responsibilities and qualifications in order to hold the office of a pastor.

1 This is a true saying, If a man desire the office of a bishop, he desireth a good work.

2 A bishop then must be blameless, the husband of one wife, vigilant, sober, of good behaviour, and given to hospitality, apt to teach;

3 Not given to wine, no striker, not greedy of filthy lucre; but patient, not a brawler, not covetous;

One that ruleth well his own house, having his children in subjection with all gravity;

5 (For if a man know not how to rule his own house, how shall he take care of the church of God?)

6 Not a novice, lest being lifted up with pride he fall into the condemnation of the devil.

7 Moreover he must have a good report of them which are without; lest he fall into reproach and the snare of the devil. (1st Timothy 3:1-7)

The Ministry of a Pastor

In the New Testament, the bishop was sometimes called a pastor. However, if Paul was talking about an office separate from the pastor, the qualifications for them would not be higher standards than for pastors.

The pastor must be blameless, or a man whose life and character cannot be spoken against. He must have only one wife. This scripture is not talking about a people who may have been divorced and remarried. It was the custom of the people in that part of the world to have several wives.

Paul was saying, after you are born again, this cannot be. To be a pastor, you must have only one wife.

There have been many men who have been called into the ministry, but because of their past life, and mistakes they made before they were born again, they did not fulfill their calling. This scripture was quoted out of context to them and they were told, because they were divorced and remarried, they did not qualify for a ministry office.

This is one of the reasons why God chooses, and not man. I'm not advocating divorce, but what is already done cannot be undone. If God has forgiven a person and called him into the ministry, it does not make any difference what men say.

If that person will submit himself to God, in due season God will raise him up. If God calls them justified, and qualifies them, their gift will make room for them.

The pastor will not be lazy. He will be a hard worker. That does not mean doing the work of the church, such as the cleaning. The ministry of helps should do that. However, he will spend much time in prayer and study in the Word of God.

He will prepare himself to meet the needs of others. He loves people and loves to fellowship with them. He will be a good teacher.

The pastor's life will be one that will be an example to the flock. More is expected out of him, because he is a leader.

The pastor is not to be a drinker of strong drink. Many have condoned this practice and said, "It won't hurt."

I advise people both in the ministry and the laity to leave it alone.

Paul said that the leader should not be greedy of filthy lucre. I agree with this statement. He should not lust money. This does not mean, nor even hint that a pastor should not be the same as anyone else. He should be awarded the same rights and privileges as anyone else in the body of Christ.

There is a saying that has been around a long time that probably has truth to it; "Lord, you keep him humble, and we'll keep him poor." In any case, people have felt that the pastor was not deserving, because he is a man of God. They equate poor with being humble. This is not true. I know people who are poor and are not humble. The more God has blessed me, the more humble I become.

I know many pastors today who, if they were in the business world, would be successful. Just because they are in the ministry, should this right of being successful and financially independent be taken away from them?

No. They give their time and care to the ministry just as a businessman would to his company. So as they are faithful, God will bless and prosper them.

Paul said that they should not be greedy. It's all right to have things, as long as you don't lust after, or be controlled by things. In other words, you can have things, as long as things don't have you.

Paul said a pastor could not be a novice, or one who has just been born again. He must first have some experience in living for God and knowing how to overcome. If he doesn't know how to help himself, how could he care for others and help show others the way?

The pastor should be well spoken of, both in the church and in his community. He must be a man of integrity. He must be one who faces and deals with personal responsibilities.

He should pay his bills on time. However, if there is some reason why he cannot, he should make arrangements with the people he owes as to when he can pay them. A leader must show the way, and if he will not take care of his responsibilities, then God cannot bless him.

This is very important. There have been those who have been slack in this area. If you can't take care of your own house, how can you guide the people of God?

1 And now, a word to you elders of the church. I, too, am an elder; with my own eyes I saw Christ dying on the cross; and I, too, will share his glory and his honor when he returns. Fellow elders, this is my plea to you:

2 Feed the flock of God; care for it willingly, not grudgingly; not for what you will get out of it, but because you are eager to serve the Lord.

3 Don't be tyrants, but lead them by your good example,

4 and when the Head Shepherd comes, your reward will be a never-ending share in his glory and honor. (1st Peter 5:1-4 Living)

Here again is an example for a pastor to be a server, and that he is to it with a willing heart. He is not to begrudge the time and energy he gives to the ministry. He is to feed the flock of God with good food.

If you are called to be a pastor, be faithful in all things. God will reward you.

As long as man is here on earth, Satan will attack any man of God. However, if he has led a life that is above reproach, he will shake off any false accusations made against him. He will go on, because he knows who he is in Christ.

There are times when it is hard to take. But a pastor must have a good reputation, both with his community and the body of Christ. When he makes some unpopular decisions, Satan tries to bring strife by blinding the eyes of some to the truth, or the true intent of the decision.

The result is that people tend to gossip and leave the church. This causes the pastor's heart to be filled with pain, because he was doing the best he knew how. Satan then begins to tell the pastor that no one loves him or appreciates him. Even though his emotions scream out at him, a real leader will get up and go on with God's business even if he has made a mistake.

Pastors are God-appointed leaders of the local church, and God Himself will see to it that the pastor's name and record are cleared in the long run.

Everyone knows that there have been people in the ministry for their own selfish gain. Some of these people have taken advantage of congregations. But just because there have been those who have gotten into error, robbed the sheep, and have beaten rather than encouraged them, you can't mistrust every pastor.

Don't put them all in the same category. Give others a chance, and let them lead you into green pastures. They can't lead you if you won't trust them enough to follow them.

The shepherd follows Jesus, and you have a responsibility of your own not to take everything that you hear at face value. Check it out with the Word of God, and if it is not of God, do not receive it. Don't give your will to anyone except God.

1 Woe be unto the pastors that destroy and scatter the sheep of my pasture! saith the Lord.

2 Therefore thus saith the Lord God of Israel against the pastors that feed my people; Ye have scattered my flock, and driven them away, and have not visited them: behold, I will visit upon you the evil of your doings, saith the Lord. (Jeremiah 23:1-2)

God is saying here that He will deal with the ones who have hurt or taken advantage of His people. It may seem like they are getting by with the wrong that they have done, but their sins will find them out.

11 I am the good shepherd: the good shepherd giveth his life for the sheep.

The Power Of God's Character

> *12 But he that is an hireling, and not the shepherd, whose own the sheep are not, seeth the wolf coming, and leaveth the sheep, and fleeth: and the wolf catcheth them, and scattereth the sheep.*
>
> *13 The hireling fleeth, because he is an hireling, and careth not for the sheep.*
>
> *14 I am the good shepherd, and know my sheep, and am known of mine.* (John 10:11-14)

The pastor who is called and appointed of God will invest his life in the ministry. He will thank God for the opportunity to serve. Those who are hirelings and not really called into the ministry will not protect the flock. They will not watch out for the wolves. The hireling feels no responsibility whatsoever for the flock.

The real pastor will invest is life to his flock. His commitment to his call is not temporary, it is until Jesus comes. He does not take it lightly, and he holds nothing back.

He knows that he cannot come and go when there are problems, because God called him there, not man. So he can't just leave anytime.

God has put a special anointing upon the pastor. Thousands of Word churches have been started in the past several years. Many of them have grown to enormous size. It is supernatural. It has not been the ability of a man or just a good team. It has been God pouring out His Spirit.

There has been great evidence of this outpouring in the ministry of a pastor. I believe you will see more and more large churches and pastors with special anointings upon them.

In many of the large conventions and campmeetings, it has been pastors who have been in demand.

Why is that?

Because people today are looking to identify with someone living a practical Christian life, not the attainment of lofty goals. And no one better exemplifies this than a pastor.

A pastor must not have his hands tied by a board where he cannot be free to do what God wants him to do. God called him and sent him to that particular city to bring light, revelation, and teaching, and to shepherd the flock. It includes the elders and deacons.

He is to be led by God, not by men and boards. He should take counsel, but it should be with those of his own level, not from someone who has a carnal mind, no vision, and is afraid to trust God. Those who would be qualified to counsel the pastor would be those who have his same qualifications.

I have made mention several times in this book not to get your eyes on the man. Beware when a pastor will not share his pulpit with the apostle, prophet and evangelist from time to time. Those with whom he shares it should have recognized ministries and be approved by other ministries of integrity. Paul said,

Be ye followers of me, even as I also am of Christ. (1st Corinthians 11:1)

Remember them which have the rule over you, who have spoken unto you the word of God: whose faith follow, considering the end of their conversation. (Hebrews 13:7)

Don't follow men, but follow their faith.

Obey them that have the rule over you and submit yourselves: for they watch for your souls, as they that must give account, that they may do it with joy, and not with grief: for that is unprofitable for you. (Hebrews 13:17)

The word "obey" comes from the Greek word "peitho," which means to trust, have confidence, believe, or agree. The word "rule" comes from the Greek word "hegeomai," which means to lead of command, with official authority.

This scripture paraphrased would read like this:

Trust and have confidence, believe and agree with them that lead with official authority, to act as a shepherd with governing powers. For they are watching for and protecting you, and they must give an account.

All men and women of God will stand before God for the way in which they have stewarded their ministry. A true pastor will lead his sheep with joy, not grief.

The pastor or shepherd must be trusted before a person is able to receive from him. A pastor should not be compared to or judged by another man, only by the Word of God.

If a person has had a bad experience, he should not hold the pastor at arms length and be afraid that he will be hurt again. The qualifications have been given by the Word for a man of God. When you see him doing what the Word says, you can trust him. Remember, always be committed and loyal to him, as he is committed and loyal to God.

God calls and appoints him to be the overseer of the local church. If he is chosen and appointed by men for this position and not by the Holy Spirit, it is possible that he will not give one hundred percent of himself.

It is difficult for him to do so, because he is always laboring under the direction of people, and not the Holy Spirit.

God calls and ordains the pastor, who in turn ordains the elders, deacons and the ministry of helps. All are submissive to his call and anointing and come under his leadership. They support him and help him carry out the vision.

Chapter 26

THE MINISTRY OF THE TEACHER

And he gave some, apostles; and some, prophets, and some, evangelists; and some, pastors; and some teachers. (Ephesians 4:11)

The ministry gift of the teacher is no less important to the body of Christ than the other four ministry gifts. When the comparison of the five ministry gifts is made to a hand, the teachers position is that of the little finger. It balances the hand. So it is with the ministry of the teacher. He brings and keeps balance in the body of Christ.

Jesus was the greatest teacher who was ever upon the earth. His teaching was simple and easy to follow and understand. He used parables to illustrate his messages.

There are people who say, "I love to hear Brother so & so, he is deep in the Word."

It may be that he spends a lot of time studying the Word, and he should. Second Timothy 2:15 says to study to show yourself approved. But this should not make his message hard to understand.

A teacher explains the Word and simplifies it. He makes it easy to understand. He brings it to a level that even a child can understand.

A revelation reveals, uncovers, or makes plain. A teacher's ministry will reveal truth to you which you did not get on your own. The teacher reads the Word, tells what it means, clarifies truth, uses terms and illustrations which can be easily understood. He applies it to everyday situations of the people.

24 And the servant of the Lord must not strive; but be gentle unto all men, apt to teach, patient,

25 In meekness instructing those that oppose themselves; if God peradventure will give them repentance to the acknowledging of the truth;
(2nd Timothy 2:24-25)

Paul was saying here that teachers must be humble and gentle with people. They cannot have an argumentative attitude, if they want people to hear and receive the Word.

A teacher will have great patience. Because many people have been taught false doctrines and are confused, he must be gentle and patient. As a result, they will be more apt to listen to him and turn to the truth.

I have always admired Norvel Hayes' compassion, humility, and patience. There was a time when God used

The Ministry of a Teacher

him to minister to me. Once when we were riding on an airplane, and he shared something with me.

He began to cry and say some things over and over to me. The Spirit of God was upon him, and the things he said seemed to go right inside of me. He demonstrated so much patience to me that it was a life-changing experience.

When Norvel teaches, he reads a scripture, and then tells an example to illustrate what he has said. He keeps saying it until his audience gets his instructions.

Beware lest any man spoil you through philosophy and vain deceit, after the tradition of men, after the rudiments of the world, and not after Christ. (Colossians 2:8)

The teacher will teach the uncompromised truth. His message and instruction will not be traditions, philosophies, thoughts or ideas of men, which produce no life or joy.

He will teach about Jesus Christ, and his message will bring unity to the body of Christ. It will not be bondage or stark law that must be adhered to. His ministry will show you how the grace of God is available to all men.

His message will not be one of condemnation, but of true love, which will open your eyes and show you who you are in Jesus Christ. He will instruct you in righteousness and how to apply the Word.

In 1972, I began taking flight instructions. My instructor was rough and abrasive if I made a mistake. He knew much more that I did. He should have, as he was the instructor and I was the student.

Because of his attitude, I could not learn from him. He made everything seem so difficult. I thought, "This is too hard, and I'll not even try to learn how to fly."

Instead, I decided I should hire another flight instructor, which I did. He was one of great experience and patience. His words were gentle, and when I failed to understand something, he went over it again. He demonstrated so much patience that he made me want to learn. He made it look so easy. In just three hours, I was taking my solo flight.

I became confident in my ability to fly the airplane, as he gave me instruction. When I went up with the flight examiner for my check ride, he told me,

"Sir, I can see that you have been taught well."

It was more than a job to the instructor who was giving me my instructions. He loved flying and he loved sharing what he had learned about it with me.

But we were gentle among you, even as a nurse cherisheth her children." (1st Thessalonians 2:7)

The God-called and God-appointed teacher will be gentle and will express the kind of love that gives you the desire to learn. Paul compared it here to the way a mother would teach and train her children.

The teacher will expose false doctrine and false teachers. His approach to this issue will not be putting others down to build himself up, but rather, taking the Word of God with love, and revealing truth.

The teacher will have the respect of the other ministry gifts. He will teach them, and he will have a teachable spirit. The ministry gift of the teacher has been more noticed in latter years. The teacher's ministry has brought great revelation and balance to the body of Christ.

If you are not called to teach, don't try to fill this office. It won't work. Stay in your calling and God will bless you where you are.

If at some time God moves you to the position of a teacher, fill it willingly and steward it well.

I am a licensed pilot, approved by the F.A.A. I know how to fly an airplane. But I am not an instructor. I have not taken the training to be one. I do not desire to be one. There is a big difference in being a pilot and being an instructor.

You do not become qualified to be a teacher just because you know the Word and have gone to Bible School and prepared yourself.

If God does not call you, you are not a teacher. Knowing the Word does not give you a right to teach.

The ministry of the teacher is a special gift to which God gives a very special anointing. Some have revelation in one area, and some in another. God gives the body everything that they need when they need it. Thank God for giving us the teacher and all the ministry gifts.

The Power Of God's Character

I have poured out my soul to you in this book, sharing with you many of my personal experiences in life and in the ministry. My desire is that you have received revelation from these personal examples, and that you will be able to apply many things from this book to your life and ministry.

I have not intended to make it sound negative, or lead you to believe, if you apply enough works, you will be good enough to be used of God by the gifts of the Spirit or be called into one of the five ministry gifts.

No, not at all. I understand God's grace and His gifts, and he gives them to whom He pleases.

In many years in the ministry I have seen error. Those who have been in the ministry for personal gain are in error. Those who went out without a foundation are in error. There have been men with great ministries who have been deceived. They have gotten their eyes on themselves and have become puffed up. When they fell, many people were hurt.

I want you to know the truth, and how to walk in it, and how to watch for yourself.

I thank God for the ministry He has given to me. I also thank God for the privilege of working with and beside some of the great men of God. It has been a great advantage to me.

Notes

Notes

Notes

Notes